Successful Parenting Workbook

create your custom plan for raising independent children into adulthood

Table of Contents

Dedication

We dedicate this workbook to families with whom we have worked.
Through their processes, we have grown as clinicians.

Acknowledgments

This workbook, the first in a series, is a work of love and respect. Respect for one another as professionals, respect for our clients, and respect for the power of improvement, especially improving what matters most - relationships. We love our work. We love when parents learn and grow, and gain confidence in themselves. It is rewarding for us to watch families open themselves to new ways of learning and practice.

We would not be writing and publishing about our professional passion of empowering families to be healthy without our wonderful foundations in education and training, significant support, and encouragement along the way. We would like to make special mention of our cohort at AMITA Health Alexian Brothers Behavioral Health Hospital, Hoffman Estates where we worked for a combined 25 plus years. Much of this time was spent with program development, leading parenting workshops and groups, providing family sessions, and working with children and adolescents. We are grateful for these opportunities, as they have allowed us growth as clinicians. We would like to thank all the school districts, and professional and educational organizations who have invited us to provide parent universities, staff trainings, and consultation. These experiences have been invaluable in our research into and understanding of parent coaching, which has taught us what works with real families.

We would like to thank our editor Mary Howenstine. She not only edited our workbook, but also provided us guidance, support and encouragement along the way. Under the creative guidance and inspiration of Lynn Kupczyk, our work came to life. Special mention goes to Sarah VanMoffaert who assisted us with editing, proofing and creative design ideas.

Introduction

For the past 25 years, our work has focused on supporting parents in their efforts to raise healthier children. We work with families to develop deeper connections, to achieve family value-driven goals, and to empower parents to feel more confident in their skills. Much in this workbook comes directly from the journey that we have walked with these families.

This workbook serves as a guide to:
- Help you reflect on your current parenting strategies
- Help you find ways to identify and create goals
- Activate the strategies needed to meet your goals

The fact that you are reading this workbook says that you are invested in your child. So, welcome! You may be using this workbook in a workshop or reading it on your own; either way, you have taken the first step. You have resources. You are not alone.

Keep in mind that your child is always evolving and there is no perfect, together child. Despite the myths in media, particularly social media, all children struggle at different points during their development. In fact, it can be during the most frustrating difficulties that true, lasting social and emotional growth occurs. Growth is on-going, during both good times and hard times. Parents do not have to wait for turmoil or difficulties to initiate change.

As parents, teachers, and caregivers, we often remind children and adolescents, "YOU ARE ENOUGH, not because of how well you perform, but because of who you are." You, too, are enough, not because of how well you perform, but because of who you are. Please be mindful of self-critical thinking and self-judgment. Use this guide to help you recognize, then strengthen, new or current strategies to parenting. Let this workbook solidify your feelings of worth.

> *"There is no such thing as a perfect parent. So just be a real one."*
>
> *~ Sue Atkins (Atkins, n.d.)*

We hope this workbook provides you with an opportunity to reflect, grow, and learn more about yourself as a parent. We purposely created a simplistic and tangible approach. Do not scrap all your parenting techniques. Incorporate what you learn into your current parenting style. As your instincts meld with healthy strategies, you will foster a more emotionally strong, confident, and resilient child.

How to Use this Workbook

Our model consists of five levels. Whether you are a mental health or educational professional, a parent, or both, we hope this is a useful guide in developing a plan to meet your individualized needs. As you work through this workbook, you will be developing your own family plan by reflecting, journaling, answering questions, and completing worksheets. Each child develops at a different rate and will approach emotional milestones at their own unique pace. While this model can be utilized with children facing all different challenges, consider those unique needs of the child in the assessment and goal stage, as well as when implementing the plan. This workbook is not meant to be completed in one sitting. Take your time, and allow yourself the opportunity to reflect and process your experience.

Disclaimer: This material is designed to provide information about the subject matter covered. We provide this information with the understanding that neither the authors nor any contributors are giving mental health, professional, or legal advice of services within the material. If expert assistance, legal services, or counseling are needed, the reader should find and use the services of licensed professionals in their jurisdiction. The authors assume no responsibility for any damages incurred as a result of using this information. The names of certain individuals were changed to protect their privacy. The Emotional Development Scale was developed by coalescing several theorist models, such as Piaget, Erikson, Watson, Skinner, Bowlby, Bandura and our own experience. If your child struggles with developmental delays, this scale may not accurately reflect his/her emotional development. We encourage you to take into consideration any special circumstances that may impact the assessment phase and goal setting for your child.

A Dictionary? Really?

Yes, really. Well, not really. It is more a glossary of terms that may have different or fuller meanings in the context of parenting philosophy. Think of the terms as tools you need in your parenting toolbox. Knowing what the terms mean will help you navigate this workbook. Do not use the wrong tool! Basically, do not use a measuring tape when you need a level.

"Strike and struggle precede success, even in the dictionary."

~Christian Slater (Smith, 2014)

Glossary

Assess
An ongoing process aimed at exploring oneself or others to improve an understanding of values, behaviors, actions, attitudes, and experiences.

Cognitive
Cognitive is relating to, being, or involving conscious intellectual activity (such as thinking, reasoning, or remembering).

Emotion
A natural instinctive state of mind deriving from one's circumstances, mood, or relationships with others.

Emotional Reactivity
An emotional response to an event, where individuals may have varying intensity of emotion. The speed to reach the emotion and return to the baseline of the emotion is described as fast. Many individuals recognize that the reaction is impulsive.

Example Case Study
These are vignettes, or glimpses, of client situations created to explain a practice, process, or philosophy. Information has been altered to protect the identities of families. No identifying information is included in any example.

Functional
How something operates, works, or organizes its surroundings. The desired outcome of function is usefulness.

Goals or Outcome Goals
The desired big picture result.

Modeling
Observational learning or imitation. Parents demonstrate behaviors, thoughts or attitudes that they want their children to copy.

Outcome Mindset

The process of staying focused on or evaluating from the end position. This is an "all or nothing" process: in or out, present or not.

Process Mindset

The process of staying focused on the path that leads to outcome. This framework of thinking helps parents recognize change and progress.

Norm

Usual, typical, or standard.

Parent(s)

Throughout this workbook, we use the word parent(s) to describe the primary caregiver. The parent may or may not be the biological parent or the individual who is called mom/dad.

Privilege

A special opportunity granted or earned.

Process

To perform a series of operations or actions to initiate change. This includes a period where change or growth occurs.

Resilience

The ability to utilize skills to recover from difficulties, bounce back from setbacks, and work through challenging situations.

Reflective Questions

These are questions to ask yourself. When you reflect, please take a few moments to think, and then choose an answer: reflect and answer. At times we provide sample answers, and other times we ask you to respond without using a sample to get you started. (The samples are examples or prompts, nothing more.) Remember, there are no wrong answers.

Sample Answers

Sample answers are answers we encountered during our work with families. There are no right or wrong answers. These are only examples, to help you begin. (We do not always provide sample answers.)

Somatic

Soma is a Greek word which means living body. Somatic refers to the mind-body connection such as when fatigue or pain is related to emotions, i.e., stomach aches or headaches brought on by emotion.

Structure

To construct or arrange according to a plan. For our purposes, structure is about creating routine or order in an environment or home. We use the terms structure and routine interchangeably.

Values

One's judgments or views as to what is important in life: "What do you hold dear to you?"

Chapter One

RESILIENCY: A PARENTING SHIFT

*"Persistence and resilience only come from having been given
the chance to work through difficult problems."*

~ Margaret Thatcher (Hutyra, n.d.)

A trending topic among mental health professionals, educators and parents is resilience. Over time, expectations of parents have changed, and parenting strategies have altered as new norms formed. A parenting norm is what society expects from parents.

The effectiveness of current parenting norms, in comparison to those of previous generations, is up for debate. Did parenting strategies from decades ago create greater self-reliance in children? Did those children experience more circumstances in which they were told to sit with distress and subsequently learn to manage hurt feelings themselves? Some argue in prior generations, children were allowed more unstructured and unsupervised time, which, in turn, increased opportunities for children to problem-solve, discover, and learn to manage conflict (Barron, C., 2016). Have parenting strategies shifted to focus increasingly on protection, structure, and comfort? Why does it seem the current generations of children appear less emotionally mature than ever before?

Laura Berk (Berk, 2013), a child development expert, provides a perspective on managing emotions. "Your emotion," she writes, "is a rapid appraisal of the personal significance of the situation, which prepares you for action. For example, happiness leads you to approach, sadness to passively withdraw, fear to move away actively, and anger to overcome obstacles." An emotion, then, expresses your readiness to establish, maintain, or change your relationship to the environment on a matter of importance to you (Campos, Frankel, & Camras, 2004; Saarni et al., 2006). In fact, a number of theorists take a functionalist approach to emotion, emphasizing that the broad function of emotions is to energize behavior aimed at attaining personal goals. When emotional maturity is lacking, children may struggle to interact appropriately with their environments, and problems can manifest in many aspects of their day-to-day lives.

Another potential reason for this shift in emotional maturity may be due to established trends toward increased emphasis on "fairness" and avoidance of hurt feelings, especially for younger children. Societal changes have had a significant impact on these trends. Many parents find themselves with an increased focus on safety, comfort, and happiness, but question if this increased focus is contributing to less self-reliance. Parents and educators emphasize the idea that every child should be treated "fairly." A common argument manifests in "participation trophies" or awards granted regardless of achievement. The rationale is that inclusive, rather than exclusive, awards, avert hurt feelings, foster the confidence and happiness of each child, and promote "fairness." Are these notions genuinely fair? And more importantly, are they beneficial?

In addition to changes in parenting styles over time, research also tells us that the increased use of technology and the reconstruction of societal expectations for children has led to changes, both in the educational system as well as in family life. We often hear from school districts that they are struggling to meet the mental health needs of their students. Some school districts place great emphasis on assessment scores and advanced placement classes, only to find increased stress and anxiety among their students. Within any given classroom, there is a diverse student population with a broad spectrum of needs and origins of stress. Moreover, some districts lack resources to provide interventions and support for students.

Every child will face stressors and challenges unique to their situation. We have observed some children are more scheduled than any previous generation of children, overscheduled even, and expectant of instant gratification. We have also seen some children have a hard time finding motivation and their place in the classroom. Some families we work with also struggle to meet basic financial needs, and home life is filled with high stress. The students who have experienced high stress, whether internal or external, are more prone to have mental health needs, which require additional resources. Educators have shared with us that those students who find it difficult to self-motivate, or appear apathetic to education, may in fact be struggling to connect in school or home setting.

While we do not have all the answers, we do know parents and school personnel frequently ask us for ways to help children manage their stress, and to learn strategies to cope. We hope you find guidance from this workbook.

Every child will face stressors and challenges
unique to their situation.

Overview

The parenting approach we recommend is for parents to start with an identified foundation, then develop and build a model of action that is individualized and based on their family's value-driven goals. Every family is unique; each plan will look different.

"I love it when a plan comes together."

~ Colonel John "Hannibal" Smith, played by actor George Peppard, The A-Team

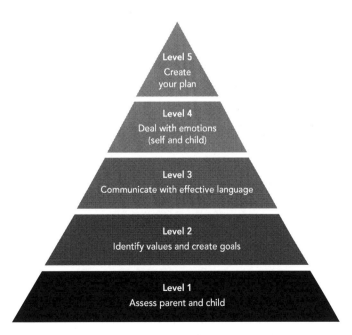

Level 5
Create
your plan

Level 4
Deal with emotions
(self and child)

Level 3
Communicate with effective language

Level 2
Identify values and create goals

Level 1
Assess parent and child

Chapter Two

LEVEL 1: ASSESS PARENT AND CHILD

"Anyone can plot a course with a map or compass; but without a sense of who you are, you will never know if you are already home."

~ *Shannon L. Alder (Alder, n.d.)*

In Level 1 (Assess Parent and Child), you will reflect on your skills, core beliefs, and assumptions, based on your history and individual development. The assessment asks you to look at your child, not from the perspective of the child's parent, but as an outsider who is assessing your child's strengths and limitations. The assessment of your child's emotional development is core to the process. Although it is important to know and understand the entire story, it is not helpful during the assessment phase to get caught up in the explanation or reason for why a child is at a particular stage in development. The "why" may only encourage enabling of the child. Your first task, then, is a bit challenging; step back a bit and take inventory of your child's development.

Parenting philosophies and skills do not just surface when we become parents. They are shaped by observing our parents' style and of course, from personal childhood experiences. Our parents' reactions to pivotal and traumatic events during our own childhoods play a role in how we learn to respond to our own children, particularly in times of difficulty and stress.

When parents become familiar with parenting styles, they can recognize and label how they were parented, as well as see their own patterns of behavior. Sometimes, when the topic of development of styles arises, some parents insist, "I am nothing like my parents. Nothing." They do not want to go there. It is understandable and common to avoid or even deny having similarities to your own parents. It can be uncomfortable, for a variety of reasons. You must trust the process. Seeing similarities (and dissimilarities) in parenting is very important for your growth as an aware, capable parent. Initial discomfort is worth the gains that come with this very personal self-awareness exercise.

Author Daniel Siegel (2001) explains how people duplicate familiar paths or styles. You are walking to a body of water, with no pathways, and you must forge through a field of high grass. As you walk, the grass beneath your feet bends, and a natural path is created. On your way to and from the water, the trail becomes more established. The next day you visit again, and you walk the same path. For the next five days, you walk the path to visit the water. A pattern is created. Siegel explains our neurons work similarly. Neurons (essential brain nerve cells) tend to flow in an established pattern.

What is even more interesting is that if you come back to the water years later, you are more likely to follow a similar pathway. Have you ever returned to your childhood home and all the siblings automatically grab their childhood dinner table places? Or, without thinking, you find yourself perched on a long outgrown stool that was your spot as a child?

Hara Estroff Morano (2010), in her *Psychology Today* blog on siblings, refers to falling into our family roles after being away as the "Thanksgiving Effect." Although we no longer live at home, when we return, we often react using our old paths. This is a reasonable explanation as to why we use language and actions we promised we would never use with our own children.

Example Case Study

A father joined his son for a counseling session. The father's goal was to improve communication with his son. The father had a revelation when he reflected on his parenting reactions. He noticed that some of his responses were influenced by his own childhood experiences. This father stated, "I bet this is why I am so quick to anger. My father often used extreme anger and at times physical aggression. I always thought I was doing a better job since I do not use physical force. My quick temper and yelling is hurting my relationship with my son. I am teaching him unhealthy ways to respond to anger." A huge, painful revelation but one that changed him as a parent forever.

Reflective Questions

1. Write down words you would use to describe yourself as a parent.
   (Sample answers: loving, impatient, exhausted, worried, and committed)

....

....

....

2. List your parenting strengths: those qualities you appreciate about yourself and would like to keep.
   (Sample answers: loving, proud)

....

....

....

3. List what you want to improve, change or learn as a new parenting skill.
   (Sample answers: I would like to be calmer and confident about my parenting. I want to see how I am doing a good job)

....

....

....

Now, go back in time and reflect on your childhood. Close your eyes, be still, and let the thoughts come. Take notice of how your parents responded to you and your siblings and what prompted action. What pops into your head? Remember, there are no right or wrong answers. Just identify your first thoughts about your own upbringing. Although this exercise may be challenging, understanding a bit about how you were raised is beneficial. Perhaps you, for the first time, can understand what you may or may not be unconsciously modeling.

....

....

....

....

....

....

....

....

Clients' Reflections on Their Childhoods

Our parents did not eat dinner with us. We had the same bedtime every night. My mom had simple routines. Our grandparents got us off to school. Doing well in sports was very important at our house.

Parenting Styles:
The Balance Between Support and Control

Increasing Support →

The Permissive Parent
is highly supportive but makes few rules and trusts rather than monitors.

"I trust you'll do the right thing."

The Authoritative Parent
is highly supportive AND monitors and sets rules.

"I care, and I'll give you the freedoms you earn: but, for safety-related issues, you'll do as I say."

The Uninvolved Parent
sets few rules, does not monitor, and offers little active support.

"Kids will be kids - you'll learn from your mistakes."

The Authoritarian Parent
sets many rules and closely monitors but offers little support.

"You'll do as I say."

Increasing Control →

(Note: Parenting styles are fluid and not always consistent. It is critical to understand many factors within the family: the needs and personality of the child, adult relationships, living conditions, jobs, extended family, and other family stressors impact parenting. Your parenting style, indeed everyone's parenting style, will fluctuate. Take a moment to familiarize yourself with parenting styles on the chart above.)

Identify your parenting styles and recognize when your style shifts.

....

....

....

....

....

....

....

....

Reflective Questions

What parenting style do these famous TV parents employ?

Marie Romano (Everyone Loves Raymond): ....

Gloria Delgado-Pritchett (Modern Family): ....

Mitchell Pritchett (Modern Family): ....

Jay Pritchett (Modern Family): ....

Aunt Viv (Fresh Prince of Bel Air): ....

Lorelai Gilmore (Gilmore Girls): ....

Belita Moreno (The George Lopez Show): ....

Lucious Lyon (Empire): ....

Cookie Lyon (Empire): ....

Example Case Study

In a family we worked with, the parents had opposing styles, authoritarian and permissive, so arguments often erupted between the parents.

During the second counseling session, the authoritarian parent started to talk about the need to counter the permissive parent. The dialogue shifted to a greater reflection of childhood experiences. During the process, the permissive parent recognized that his parent's style was often authoritarian. Desiring to have the children experience a different childhood, the parent utilized more permissive parenting. The use of permissive style was strengthened when the opposing parent employed an authoritarian approach.

In short, as this couple began to understand their parenting styles and recognized how childhood experiences influence their parenting styles, the couple created a more consistent and purposeful approach to managing their child's behaviors. The household stabilized.

(Note: Sometimes factors such as mental health or substance abuse impact parenting styles and the ability to effectively parent. If this is a concern, please consult a professional provider.)

Another Perspective on Assessment

"When I took the time to identify and label the parenting I received, I was able to be objective about my own parenting in a way that I never dreamed I could. I could see where I was not focusing on what was best for my child. I was not aware I was pulling techniques from my childhood. My parenting became more deliberate when I could acknowledge without judgment how I was parented."

~ Suzie, single mother of 3

Creating Your Time Line

Next, we encourage you to create a time line for reflection. Your time line is built of different events or memories, from delightful moments to those you may find difficult to process. Think of the time line as a rearview mirror of your childhood. Your time line allows you to view the milestones that record your journey to parenthood. By completing the time line, you can reflect on how the recorded events, and their significance, impact your parenting style.

Below write down any and all childhood memories. Do not be concerned about placing these into chronological order. Chronology, or sequence, will be addressed next. Do not be concerned with spelling or grammar. Just get the memories recorded.

Now, We Will Begin to Create a Time Line

Start with the year you were born.

Using the notes you jotted on the previous pages, use the Time Line Worksheet on the following pages to rearrange in chronological order (to the best of your ability) your memories.

For each entry
a. Write a summary of significant events.
b. Include facts such as who was involved and the impact of the event.
c. At each point of memory, identify parenting tactics that your parents used (silent treatment, yelling, grounding).
d. What parenting style did they use (authoritarian, authoritative, passive, uninvolved)?
e. Make a note to indicate if parenting styles changed or remained consistent.
f. Can you remember how your parent(s) or caregiver(s) responded?
g. What do you think your parent(s) or caregiver(s) were attempting to accomplish?
h. Were they calm, or did they become emotional? Did your parent(s) or caregiver(s) impulsively respond?
i. Add any details that help you tell your narrative.
j. Finally, identify which of your earlier childhood memories impact how you parent today.

Note: If you recognize or suspect, or, yes, fear, your childhood experiences are traumatic or difficult to process, seek support to complete this exercise.

YOUR TIME LINE WORKSHEET

Utilize the worksheet to create a timeline of memories from childhood

Example

1992

7 YO: Dad didn't let me snack when I was hungry.

I was alone with my dad and he was watching a baseball game. I was playing and decided to get a snack without asking. He yelled at me to spit it out and put it back. Very authoritarian parenting style. I later understood this did not keep me from eating between meals, and I became more rebellious as a teenager due to this continuous parenting style. As a parent, I do not want this for my children.

(continues on the next page)

Next, look at awareness, from both an internal (self) and external (social) perspective. Developing self-awareness is not about having an in-depth exploration of your innermost thoughts or feelings, it is about knowing yourself and understanding your pressure points. Self-awareness is beneficial in creating a purposeful parenting strategy.

Reflective Questions

1. What drives you?

(Sample answers: My love for my children, competition. I have no support system and must be self-reliant, I must be strong.)

....

....

....

2. What do you react to in others?

(Sample answers: I react strongly to dishonesty; I respond positively to someone who cares and takes action.)

....

....

....

In Emotional Intelligence 2.0., Bradberry and Greaves (2012) discuss two keys to emotional intelligence, Personal Competence and Social Competence. Self-awareness and self-management are subcategories of Personal Competence. Social Competence also has two subcategories, social management and relationship management. Understanding these keys helps the parent to assess their own level of emotional intelligence and skills to create growth opportunities for their child. **Think of it in this way, when you are working with someone that appears confident, you feel more secure and safe in making mistakes and taking risks.**

When you are working with someone that appears confident,
you feel more secure and safe in making mistakes and taking risks.

Personal Competence (Self-Awareness and Self-Management)

Personal competence is the self-awareness of, and management of, one's own emotions when faced with everyday trials and tribulations.

Management of emotions does not mean to avoid or ignore the emotions occurring, but rather to identify, experience, and respond in a manner that is effective and purposeful. Being able to experience emotions and model effective ways to manage is valuable for children to experience. We will touch more on modeling emotions later in this workbook.

Management of emotions does not mean to avoid or ignore
the emotions occurring, but rather to identify, experience, and respond
in a manner that is effective and purposeful.

A person is self-aware AND manages his/her own emotions when he/she anticipates reactions and plans reasonable and healthy responses.

A Parent's Perspective on Personal Competence

"I know debating politics on social media frustrates me, so I am not going to test my self-control. I am just not going to read my friends' political posts."

~ Shannon, mother of 3

Reflective Questions

1. Identify an emotion that you often experience when dealing with your child.
   (Sample answers: frustration, guilt, joy, anger, etc.)

   ....

   ....

   ....

   ....

2. Identify a time that you were experiencing an intense emotion and feel proud about the way you handled the situation.
   (Sample answer: I was really frustrated with my son's behavior, but removed a privilege without yelling or power struggling with him.)

   ....

   ....

   ....

   ....

"When you take the time to listen, with humility, to what people have to say, it is amazing what you can learn. Especially if the people who are doing the talking also happen to be children."

~ Greg Mortenson, (Mortenson, 2010)

Social Competence (Social Awareness and Relationship Management)

Social competence involves understanding your child's experience from his/her perspective and reacting in a manner that strengthens the relationship by using self-awareness, self-management, and social awareness. Social awareness involves the use of empathy to understand what others might be experiencing and how others respond to situations.

(Note: empathy, not to be confused with sympathy, is the ability to understand and share the feelings of another, rather than feeling sorry for the individual.)

Example Case Study

In one family we worked with, the parents felt that the child did not take responsibility for choices. The parents started to believe that their child lacked remorse, which increased the parents' frustration and suspicion that they were being taken advantage of. Often the child would defend her actions, and the parents would go into a monologue. "If you would do this or that, blah, blah" or "It is so simple." As the parents gained social competency, they began to understand their child was experiencing shame. The parents shifted their responses and language.

The most powerful piece in the process of the change was having the parents recognize how their interpretation of the child's experience impacted responses. By saying less and increasing simple empathetic responses, the parents created an atmosphere where the child was able to experience his/her emotional responses. The child spoke more and, revealed more. This allowed the parents to challenge the critical self-talk that the child often used. The child reported that he/ she felt validation from the parents. Both parents and child found that they experienced fewer arguments, but more importantly, their bond grew stronger.

Another Perspective on Social Competence

"I did not become a better parent until I became a better listener. I was so busy trying to apply a solution to every problem, and I never got to the real problem. Now, I listen and listen and listen."

~ Bob, father of 1

Complete this sentence.

When my child ...., I respond with ....

Another tool to discover your listening and response skill set is the *Obstacles to Effective Parenting* Worksheet. The worksheet is intended to help you start your journey of purposeful parenting. Keep this worksheet, and use it as a working document, making changes and identifying growth during your process. Parents will discover more about their reactions and style as they shift from a reactive parenting style to purposeful parenting.

OBSTACLES TO EFFECTIVE PARENTING WORKSHEET

Describe specific situations related to your children that make you feel varying levels of discomfort. On a scale of 0 to 10 (0 being very comfortable, and 10 being extremely uncomfortable), rate how much each situation affects you.

SITUATION	0 - 10

Assess Parent and Child

Things to think about while assessing your child's functioning

As therapists, when we first meet with families, we look at where the child is functioning emotionally and physically, as well as cognitively. Many parents tell us, "Our child is so bright. We are concerned that our child is having such a difficult time managing stress and meeting expectations."

Reflective Questions

1. What are three characteristics that describe your child?

....
....
....

2. What would your child say are the three characteristics that you would use to describe him/her?

....
....
....

3. Why do you think you chose those three characteristics?

....
....
....

4. Do you think these characteristics reflect the values that are important to you?

....
....
....

Often, there is a discrepancy between the emotional and cognitive levels of development. What does that mean exactly? A child who is very intelligent (cognitive label) but seems immature or acts out defiantly (emotional label) may confuse and frustrate the parent(s).

(Note: We do not look at the children as mentally ill or challenging. We assess where they are in terms of their cognitive and emotional development, and work with parents to create and assess strategies that will help to close the gap and raise their emotional development to be more in line with cognitive development.)

While we will not go into detail on physical development, this is another aspect to think about, since this may impact performance, as well as how others respond to the child. For instance, if a child is twelve, but looks fifteen, others may place expectations on the child, reacting to the child as if he/she were fifteen rather than twelve with appropriate twelve-year-old behavior.

In this next section, we take a closer look at the differences between emotional development and cognitive functioning.

Emotional Development

Emotional development is "the emergence of a child's experience, expression, understanding, and regulation of emotions from birth through late adolescence. It also comprises how growth and changes in these processes concerning emotions occur" (Oolup, 2015). Emotional development includes the ability to manage emotions using skills such as distress tolerance, communication, conflict resolution, and self-soothing, as well as meeting the milestones associated with one's age. It is critical for people to recognize, communicate, and manage emotions in a healthy way. Emotional development incorporates skills which must be fostered over time; therefore, it is essential to recognize appropriate expectations for children of various age groups.

Cognitive Functioning

Cognitive functioning looks at one's mastery of the skills required to learn, gain, and process new information, problem solve, and remember and retrieve information (https://sharpbrains.com/blog/2013/04/18/what-is-their-combined-effect-of-physical-and-mental-training/).

Cognitive ability and mastery of academic skills are measured by testing instruments and other evaluation measures both within and out of the school setting. The data gathered from these measures are often used to determine class placement and other expectations for academic performance. Emotional development is separate from cognitive development; therefore, discrepancies may exist between a child's emotional and cognitive levels. For example, a child may be advanced in his/her cognitive development but have not yet reached the emotional developmental milestones for his/her age group. An awareness of a child's emotional and cognitive levels is crucial to implementing appropriate parenting and teaching strategies.

EMOTIONAL DEVELOPMENT SCALE

Many measures are available to assess a child's cognitive level, but it can be more challenging to determine a child's emotional level. **One important assessment or measure is the Emotional Development Scale.** We created this scale to look at target benchmarks, including skills and behaviors typical for each age group. This tool is a scale that gives examples of desired behaviors for each age to gauge emotional functioning. It can be used as a guide to assess an adolescent's level of emotional maturity, especially in comparison to his/her cognitive level of development. Parents and teachers can use personal experience and observations, as well as a child's self-report, to identify levels of functioning and set goals for desired emotional growth. This tool can also be helpful in establishing expectations for the child, both in the classroom and at home, and in utilizing interventions to help aid in emotional development.

One important assessment or measure is the Emotional Development Scale.

The use of the Emotional Developmental Scale has helped us gain a greater understanding of how a child functions, particularly when the child is struggling to meet expectations or manage his/her emotions. The scale may also be helpful when selecting appropriate school placement, establishing expectations, and evaluating class rigor and school schedules.

Too often, parents and teachers cling to the notion that if a child is bright, he/she should be able to handle an increased workload of rigorous classes. Depending on the emotional maturity of the child, this is not always the case.

EMOTIONAL DEVELOPMENT SCALE

Age 18: Development of personal identity and move towards independence by setting goals. Planning for future (i.e. move away from home, going to college). Being able to tolerate disappointment and increased demonstration of critical thinking skills.

Age 16: More regular use of emotional self-regulation and distress tolerance skills. Ability to think of different possible outcomes and work towards goals when approaching a problem. Identify and understand core-beliefs. Quest to start moving towards independence away from parents (i.e. driving). Experimenting with different behaviors and ideas.

Age 14: Increase in use of critical thinking skills and development of abstract thinking. Heavily influenced by peers' opinions and judgments. Self-esteem will be influenced by peers' opinions. Will advocate for needs and start/practice setting boundaries with peers. Engaging in serious aggression, is rare. Aggressive behaviors are more verbal. Recognizes that outbursts have consequences.

Age 12: Starts to develop critical thinking skills and recognition of more than the obvious answer. Increase in empathy skills and understanding that others may have mixed feelings. Concerned with peer opinions and fitting in but should be able to handle limits and calm self when upset. May become frustrated with limits, due to wanting more immediate gratification.

Age 10: Reasoning becomes logical but if unable to solve problem may ignore or redefine the situation (may appear to lack responsibility). Empathy increases as emotional understanding improves. Start to see interest/concern about peer approval and social support. Develop internal skills for managing emotion.

Age 8: An increase in development of skills to manage peer interactions and social situations. Sensitivity to criticism and struggles with failure, tendency to be competitive and bossy. Peer influence emerges, concerned about being liked by their friends. Aggression is markedly decreased or nonexistent, may see physical reaction to communicate emotions (i.e. pouting when upset). Awareness of others and consideration for other's feelings and needs, especially if other is disadvantaged (understanding of benevolence). Decrease in black and white thinking pattern, able to understand "shades of gray". Fears are less based in imaginary objects.

Age 6: Ambition and responsibility are developed, greater understanding of causes and consequences, strategies for self-control expand. Able to utilize language to manage anger and significant decrease in aggressive behaviors. Temper tantrums, yelling, blaming, arguing behaviors should decrease or abate as the emotions become more regulated and language is more utilized to express emotions.

Age 4: Empathy and problem-solving emerges. May see decline in physical aggression (hitting, fighting, throwing things, etc) although may still see irritability, blaming. During frustration may exhibit infant behaviors. Can express basic emotions (happy, sad, proud and excited).

Ages 2-3: Temper tantrums, self-centered, and immediate satisfaction is hallmark. Often says "no" and shows lots of emotions (laughs, squeals, throws things, cries). Use of external behaviors to express emotions (i.e. throwing and destroying property). Can play alone and does not need other involvement. Resists change.

© Jackie Rhew and Robin Choquette 2014

Disclaimer: The Emotional Development Scale was developed by coalescing several theorist models, such as Piaget, Erikson, Watson, Skinner, Bowlby, Bandura and our own experience. If your child struggles with developmental delays, this scale may not accurately reflect his/her emotional development We encourage you to take into consideration any special circumstances that may impact the assessment phase and goal setting for your child.

Reflective Questions

Examine the scale and try to establish your child's emotional level of functioning.

1. Does your child's level of emotional functioning change in different environments? How so?

....
....
....
....

2. Does your child's level of emotional functioning change because of external factors (i.e., stress, etc.)?

....
....
....
....

Both the emotional and cognitive levels provide a broader and more accurate picture of a child's overall level of functioning.

Example Case Study

A few years ago, we worked with a 14-year-old girl entering her freshman year of high school. This girl had scored high on her standardized tests, and it was apparent that she was profoundly cognitively intelligent. However, the girl struggled to manage stress. She was very concrete and perfectionistic in her thinking and quickly overwhelmed. When upset, she would scream, cry, and at times self-injure. The school had encouraged her to take a rigorous course load due to her impressive test scores, but she put a lot of pressure on herself to excel and became severely distressed when she did not perform to these high standards. Due to her level of emotional functioning, the intense schedule was not appropriate for this particular child and created a sense of failure. When assessing her schedule, it was important to look at her emotional functioning in addition to her cognitive abilities. Taking both factors into account, we were able to create a schedule that she could manage, allowing her to excel while continuing to gain confidence and grow emotionally.

Another Perspective on Emotional and Cognitive Development

"My son is an "old soul," a quiet thinker, reasonably bright and a good test taker. Emotionally, he was always the more mature and logical of friends his age. I recognized, eventually, that everyone (including me) expected too much of him. Although he had high-level math and science skills, he often struggled in his STEM classes. What I came to realize was that he lacked useful communication skills. He developed academically stronger when we focused on his communication skills."

~ John, father of 2

How Behaviors are Maintained

Now, we shift focus from emotions to behaviors. We believe that behaviors are maintained by reinforcement; they do not just appear or repeat. Reinforcement may occur without recognition or awareness, but spending some time looking at patterns of behavior can help you begin to assess them.

Parents have told us that it can be difficult to recognize patterns, especially when their children are displaying concerning behaviors. We often encourage parents to first recognize the behavior, then think about how others in the child's life respond to the behavior of concern. This can help understand what responses may be reinforcing the behavior. It can be especially difficult to understand patterns when children are dealing with mental health or medical issues. It is during these times that parents may be more prone to react out of emotion.

With the use of these next reflective questions, you will gain an understanding of your responses, and how the responses may reinforce behaviors. How might you be reinforcing a behavior?

Reflective Questions

1. Identify your child's behaviors that create the most concern for you.

....
....
....
....

2. Do others in your child's life express similar or different concerns? If so, please list here.

....
....
....
....

3. How do individuals in your child's life respond to concerning behavior (i.e., each parent, especially when parents differ, other caregiver(s), family members, peers, and school staff)?

....
....
....
....

4. Are concerning behaviors being reinforced? If so, how?

....
....
....
....

Assessing Functioning

In this chapter we discussed areas of development and functioning. Now it is time for you to answer a few questions to get a global picture and a better understanding of how your child functions in his/her environment.

Assessing a child's functioning can help with creating and implementing strategies and goals. Knowing your child's learning style and using strategies that align with that style will be useful and create a more harmonious environment at home.

(Note: We understand most parents are not educational psychologists or trained to give a battery of tests to evaluate a child. These assessments are informal and intended to increase parental awareness. The assessment in the next section is designed to be a tool for you, the parent, to think about your parenting and your child's development objectively. This may be the first time you have ever taken notes of this nature. Remember, do not be overly critical or analytical. Just write what you observe. These are your private notes and observations about your own child.)

We would like to introduce five areas for evaluating how your child manages. The areas are Cognitive Functioning, Emotional Functioning, Relationship/Communication, Self-Care, and Occupational. After each area, please answer the questions. Think about overarching themes and how your child generally responds. Do not over think your answers.

1. Cognitive Functioning
   a. Identify your child's learning style: visual (see), auditory (hear) or tactile (touch).

   _____

   _____

   b. Does your child need time to process information?

   _____

   _____

   c. Do you notice that your child talks through problems and situations when seeking solutions?

   _____

   _____

2. Emotional Functioning
   In this section, reference back to the <u>Emotional Development Scale</u> to help you appropriately assess your child.
   a. Can your child manage demands and expectations, or does he/she get easily overwhelmed?

   _____

   _____

   b. Does your child impulsively respond?

   _____

   _____

c. Does your child experience and demonstrate age-appropriate emotions?

....
....

3. Relationships/Communications
   a. Does your child have healthy long-lasting relationships?

....
....

   b. Can your child communicate with peers, teachers, and others to get his/her needs met, or do
      you find yourself involved?

....
....

4. Self-Care
   a. Does your child have age appropriate behaviors to meet their basic needs (i.e., does the
      adolescent rely on a parent to wake him/her every morning)?

....
....

   b. Does your child have age appropriate responsibilities to meet grooming expectations and
      nutritional and medication management, or does your child rely solely on others for reminders?

....
....

5. Occupational
   A child's occupation is being a learner at school.
   a. Does your child meet the expectations and responsibilities for coursework and the school's guidelines?

....
....

Level 1
Assess parent and child

LEVEL 1 SUMMARY

Write down your takeaways from Level 1, Assess Parent and Child.

....
....
....
....
....

Take some time to revisit the questions and your answers. Write any questions or concerns you have about your informal assessment of your parenting and your child's emotional and cognitive functioning.

....
....
....
....
....

Write a summary of what you learned about

a. Yourself

....
....
....
....
....

b. Your child

....
....
....
....
....

c. Your parenting

....
....
....
....
....

Write any questions or concerns you may want to explore more.

Chapter Three

LEVEL 2: IDENTIFY VALUES AND CREATE GOALS

It is not hard to make decisions when you know what your values are.

Roy Disney (as cited in Greathouse 2011)

Values: A person's principles or standards of behavior; one's judgment of what is important in life. The first step to identifying values is to recognize what is important to you.

Reflective Questions

1. What do you believe?
   (Sample answers: honesty, strong work ethic, intelligence, respect)

....

....

....

....

2. What really matters to you?
   (Sample answers: family being successful, financial stability, education, happiness, power, fairness)

....

....

....

....

3. What is negotiable and what is non-negotiable to you?
   (Sample answers: negotiable - happiness, power, fairness ~ non-negotiable - honesty, respect)

....

....

....

....

4. How do you want to respond to difficult situations?
   (Sample answers: I want to remain calm and provide a solution.)

....

....

....

....

5. How do you want others to see you?

(Sample answer: respectful, I want to always treat others with respect and others to treat me with respect.)

....

....

....

....

6. Now, create a list of values that are important to you.

(Sample answers: integrity, responsibility, compassion)

....

....

....

....

Once you have listed your values, join with your co-parent to identify some agreed upon family values. (We understand that this is not always possible. We will discuss co-parenting under challenging situations later.) Clarity of your family values helps navigate life. Keeping aligned to your values is essential. Think of your values as the foundation on which to build the rest of your work.

Let's say you identify family and relationships as values. Ask yourself, "Do I create opportunities to spend time with family members?" Many parents believe imparting values to their child is one of the most important responsibilities in parenting. Be warned! Talking about the family values will only get you so far. How many times has your child tuned you out and said, "Blah blah, I know, I know." **Children tend to embrace and incorporate values when they are modeled in the family.**

Children tend to embrace and incorporate values when they are modeled in the family.

Reflective Questions

1. Recount a moment that you modeled a family value.

....

....

....

....

2. What do you remember about the experience?

....

....

....

....

Example Case Study

A mother was struggling with her ten-year-old son because he would not talk to her about his day. The son would often respond with, "Nothing happened." This response would infuriate the mom, and an argument would ensue. The son soon started to avoid the mom, which increased the mom's concerns for the son. When the mom started identifying her values, she recognized that honesty was non-negotiable for her. Reflecting on her interactions with others, and in particular her son, she started to understand her response to the "nothing happened" comment. She had interpreted his response as though he was not telling her the truth and surely had something to hide. He just did not want to share the details of his day. As the mother gained awareness of her values and reactions, she learned how to decrease reactive responses. The son reported that when mom's emotional reactions dissipated, he was able to share more details. We often respond to what is important to us.

Two Perspectives on Identifying Values

"My daughter really struggles with motivation and often shuts down when feeling overwhelmed. One of our family values is hard work, so I would interpret many behaviors as laziness and failed to recognize that her motivation was impacted by her lack of self-confidence. When I shifted my language and focus to process and away from outcome, my daughter's motivation increased."

~ Rico, father of 2

"When I close my eyes and imagine my 8-year-old as an adult, I see a young person, excited about the future, with big dreams, a person who is resourceful and resilient and respectful of herself, her relationships, her environment."

~Molly, mother of 3

Reflective Questions

1. Think about your child as an adult. What type of adult are you trying to raise?

....

....

....

....

2. What are some of the characteristics you want your future adult child to have?

....

....

....

....

3. When you think about these characteristics, do your parenting strategies develop these traits?

....

....

....

....

If you are uncertain whether your strategies develop these characteristics or traits that you listed above, creating parenting goals is the first step to consciously equipping your child.

SMART Goals

SMART is a simple acronym that helps individuals create goals that are **S**pecific, **M**easurable, **A**chievable, **R**ealistic, and **T**imely. Rick Lochner's blog (http://ricklochner.com/every-obstacle-destroyed/), an author, suggests using W.A.Y.S.M.A.R.T. goals. Lochner's approach incorporates

Write goals. **A**lign goals to values. Make the goals **Y**ours.

This approach allows each family to be creative and individualized. Goals cannot be mass produced like a cookie cutter popping out perfect, identical cookies; every child's and parents' goals are unique to the child, parent, and family. Your "cookie" will be unique in every way, even though the same ingredients are used.

We really want you to feel comfortable with this exercise. You do not need to write down universal goals that every child should master, but goals that are specific to what your child needs. You want to maximize your goal setting and create your plan.

In this section, you simply create your goals. Later, you will build your family's individual plan and expectations. Start to think of your goals as your long-term aspirations for your child. You will notice we often use the term outcome goals; we encourage you to think about the outcome you are trying to create when you set your goals. Think big. Be honest! Own your dream.

Reflect. Complete this sentence.

I want my child ....

I want my child ....

I want my child ....

Sample answers:

I want my child to think I did a great job raising him or her.

I want my child to live independently and make good decisions.

I want my child to want to come home frequently when he/she is an adult.

I want my child to be free to make his/her own decisions.

I want my child to be able to camp without being homesick.

I want my child to be able to use his/her creativity to earn a living.

I want my child to be confident and healthy.

A Word About Happy and Fair

Many parents strive to make their children happy. When parents are asked to complete the statement, "I want my child to be…..." the most frequent answer is "happy." We have heard almost every parent say, "I just want my child to be happy." Some of these same children have been raised with the notion that everything should be fair. Be careful about establishing goals that incorporate "Happy and Fair."

These beliefs have made it difficult for many children to experience and work through any feelings of displeasure or discomfort. It is critical for children to learn to experience and work through frustrations, especially when the goal is maturing into a healthy young adult. It is critical because dealing with disappointment and discomfort is a part of life. We want children to understand that they can manage and experience disappointments, and as a result, further develop resiliency. **Resiliency will occur as we allow children to experience difficulties, and not shield or intervene, but provide support as they encounter discomfort and disappointments.**

Resiliency will occur as we allow children to experience difficulties, and not shield or intervene, but provide support as they encounter discomfort and disappointments.

Happiness comes from managing life, growing, overcoming obstacles, and becoming your best self. We cannot really make others happy. We can, however, give them tools to create their own happiness or feelings of self-worth.

Questions to Ask When Creating Parenting Goals

Reflective Questions

1. What would I like to teach my child through my parenting?
   (*Sample answers: I want my child to be tolerant. I want my child to set life goals.*)

....

....

....

2. What values would I like my parenting goals to reflect?
   (*Sample answer: I want to teach my child to advocate for him/herself.*)

....

....

....

3. Where would I like to see growth in my child?
   (*Sample answer: I want to see my child ask questions and not follow the crowd.*)

....

....

....

4. What are challenges I face when parenting?
   (*Sample answer: I often feel tired and have little energy.*)

....

....

....

The Miracle Question

The miracle question is a technique often used in narrative and solution-focused therapy. Answering the miracle question will allow you to envision the future and start to put words to your hopes and dreams for your child or yourself.

The miracle question: You wake up one morning, and a miracle has occurred overnight. What would be different in your or your child's life that would tell you that life is better?

Please describe below.

....

....

....

....

....

Reflective Questions

1. Identify goals for parenting (i.e., assisting your adolescent in becoming more motivated, self-confident, and independent).

....

....

....

2. Where did these goals come from?

....

....

....

3. Is there someone who can help you be accountable for these goals?

....

....

....

Supports to Help Identify Goals

Establishing goals may be new to you, or it may be something you have never explored with your child. Parents may benefit from meeting with a therapist or parenting coach to assist in developing parenting goals, as well as working on providing the child structure, consistency, and support.

When two parents are involved raising a child, it is optimal that the parents work together as a unified and consistent team. While this may not always be possible due to conflict or differing views on parenting, the child will benefit most from understanding joint parenting goals.

Support groups may be beneficial to gain extra guidance. Additional resources can often be found by contacting the school counseling office, community agencies, private practitioners, and pediatricians' offices.

LEVEL 2 SUMMARY

What are the takeaways from this Level 2, Identify Values and Create Goals? Take some time to revisit the questions and your answers.

Write any questions or concerns you may want to explore more.

Chapter Four

LEVEL 3: COMMUNICATE WITH EFFECTIVE LANGUAGE

When people talk, listen completely. Most people never listen.

Ernest Hemingway (Cowley, 1949)

Listening is a skill. Listening takes practice. There is nothing more worthwhile than investing the time in listening to your child. Not just hearing, but listening, attending, and digesting what is said.

The most basic of all human needs is the need to understand and be understood. The best way to understand people is to listen to them.

Ralph G. Nichols (Nichols, 1980)

Reflective Questions

1. Who does more talking, you or your child?
   (*Sample answer: I talk more, he avoids me.*)

....
....
....

2. How much time do you spend talking with your child each week?
   (*Sample answers: We talk every day, or we do not talk much, I feel like she avoids conversations with me.*)

....
....
....

3. Do you have regular times each week that you devote to spending time with your child/family?
   (*Sample answers: Our schedules are busy, and it is hard to have regular times each week, where everyone is available, or we spend time together each afternoon on our drive home from school.*)

....
....
....

4. What are ways to create more opportunities to engage your child?
   (*Sample answer: We try to have a game night once a week.*)

....
....
....

We talk about the use of language with parents, helping them to understand language influences the outcomes of situations. Often, assumptions are based on judgments and our emotional reactions. Assumptions also play into language choice. We will look at ways to shift our language to reflect more of our intentions and parenting goals.

Example Case Study

A father picked up his elementary school age daughter from school. The father was concerned because the daughter had been having social struggles. The father also struggles with his own anxiety. As the daughter approached the car, he became concerned that she looked sad. He asked as she entered the car, "What is wrong?" and proceeded to inquire about the situation. The daughter became increasingly upset. When meeting with the father and daughter that night, during the discussion, the father identified that they had an awful day. The daughter seemed to be in some distress and commented, "It was a terrible day."

There are a few things to learn from this example. We worked with the father on recognizing how his anxiety was impacting his parenting responses. We also worked with the father and the daughter on identifying their black-and-white thinking patterns, such as the fact that every day is a day where a lot of things happen. While some things may be more difficult to handle, there is no amazing or awful day; it is more a day filled with different occurrences. We also worked with the father on his responses as his daughter entered the car. He recognized that he could have calmly said "Hey, how was your day" or, "Tell me something that went well and something that was difficult and how you managed it." One of this father's parenting goals was to allow his daughter to experience some distress and gain confidence she could manage it. He also recognized that it was hard for him when she did not seem "happy" because he had originally parented from the mindset that his job was to make her happy. Since this was his goal, he worked on not jumping in with questions and assuming she was upset, but really focusing on being comfortable with her working out issues when they arose and not seeming upset when she was experiencing difficulties at school or with peers.

Another Perspective on Communication

"When I used less 'I should,' and 'I must,' my mood shifted from feeling inferior, and I gained confidence in my parenting skills. My consistency with limit-setting improved too!"

~Anica, mother of 5

When I used less 'I should, and 'I must,' my mood shifted from feeling inferior, and I gained confidence in my parenting skills.

Reflective Questions

1. Recognize some patterns of black and white thinking that you may have.
   (Note: black-and-white thinking, also known as all-or-none thinking, refers to rigid or concrete thinking.)
   (Sample answers: This will include all or nothing mentality: "It will always be like this. Another terrible morning.")

   ....

   ....

   ....

   ....

2. **A lot of times our children use language they learned from us.** Can you identify times when you heard your exact words spilling from your child's mouth?
   (Sample answers: words such as always, never, cannot, will not. I use the phrase "It was a terrible day." I have noticed my child uses the same words to describe a day, when he has faced a difficulty.)

   ....

   ....

   ....

   ....

A lot of times our children use language they learned from us.

3. Recognize times when you may be quick to react emotionally.
   (Sample answer: When my child fights with his brother, I tend to lose my patience and sometimes yell. Yelling is not great modeling if I am trying to teach my child how to handle conflict.)

   ....

   ....

   ....

   ....

Model for your children healthy communication patterns, and if you recognize unhealthy communication patterns exist within the family, it is ok to be transparent, especially in the hopes of making improvements. Remember not to get caught up in blame. We encourage avoiding self-deprecation. Model healthier communication styles; acknowledge the less positive. "Let me restate that in a more loving way." "I wish I had not used such emotional language."

Some children are less verbal than others, just as some parents are more talkative than others. To improve conversation with the child, **allow the child time to respond**. This may mean asking fewer questions and allowing the child time to answer, rather than interjecting or asking more questions. This can be challenging for a parent who is anxious, as well as for one who tends toward talking a lot.

Allow the child time to respond.

As we referenced in the assessment section, it will be important to be aware of the style of learning that works best for your child. It will be helpful to use language that fits with his/her type of learning. For instance, if your child is more of a visual learner, and you recognize that you do a lot of talking, you may find that your child becomes easily overwhelmed when you are talking. This is a cue to reduce talking and add more visuals or allow the child to do more of the talking.

Definitions of Learning Styles

Visual learner: Learns best with images, pictures, color and other visual media.

Auditory learner: Learns best through listening. The learner depends on hearing and speaking as a primary way of learning.

Tactile learner: Learns best by touching and doing.

Reflective Questions

1. What are some ways your child learns best (Remind yourself of your previous answer about your child's learning style, found in the assessing function area)?
   (Sample answer: My child may be more of a visual, auditory or tactile learner.)

   ....
   ....
   ....
   ....

2. Identify some ways you could shift your communication style to match your child's learning style.
   (Sample answers: I should talk less since my child is more of a visual learner. One of my children loves to mark items off the chore chart. My other child never notices there is a chore chart.)

   ....
   ....
   ....
   ....

As you figure out what type of learner your child is, think about what kinds of communication you tend to use when interacting with him/her. For example, if your child is a visual learner, you may want to do less talking. Write out expectations and use more concrete examples. Let us look at chores. For some children, the use of post-it notes might be helpful. (Be careful not to overuse the post-it note though. Overuse may lead to frustration for the child.) Maybe, place a simple reminder on a car dashboard, backpack, or the refrigerator.

The use of washable glass markers is excellent for the bathroom mirror. Gentle, not shaming, meme humor is another option. These are all great tactics for the visual learner.

(Note: We encourage the use of age-appropriate reminders. We once had a mother post a picture of how to load a dishwasher, and the adolescent found it demeaning. Can you think of any others visual reminders that would NOT be effective?)

An excellent example for a visual learner is an iconic teaching tool used in the 1970s. Watch How A BILL BECOMES A LAW: https://www.youtube.com/watch?v=l6MinvU93kI (Uber, 2013). Most every American educated baby boomer can describe the "lowly little Bill" trying to get up the hill. Grammar quiz kid or not, those same '70s educated children with a preference for auditory learning understood the functions of conjunctions because of this very basic video: https://www.youtube.com/watch?v=NWBO9NAYm-U (Riggs, R 2011). (And can probably still sing it!)

You, or your child, may have used counting cubes in the classrooms. It seems like such a common-sense thing to do now, but the manipulative is a relatively recent teaching tool. Base ten (our math system is based on tens) is a lot easier to understand for learners when they physically build using units, rods, flats, and cubes. Tactical learners are probably in "hands on" heaven in a math class that uses manipulatives to teach math concepts. The same concepts can apply at home for learning. (Ask your child if he or she used rods, flats, and cubes in math class in early elementary.)

Face-to-face, quality time is also an important aspect of family communication. We recognize that children today do not get as many face-to-face interactions as in the past. We live in a time where schedules are busy, and most of us spend a lot of time on electronics. Children need time and some undivided attention, even if they will not say it or appear interested. Attempt to work face-to-face communication time into your daily schedule. Be creative!

Brush your teeth together, develop a night time wind down routine for everyone in the family, sort and fold laundry without electronics, commit to a family puzzle or crossword puzzle for just ten minutes a night.

Example Case Study

We worked with a 9-year-old boy who reported feeling isolated and depressed. The boy's parents said that he was spending more time in his room and seemed not only to isolate himself but was irritable with family members. The parents recognized one of their goals was to connect more with their son. The parents decided to create an expectation that the son could only be in his room after 9pm and needed to spend time in the family areas until then. Electronics were more limited, and structure was added. After two weeks, the son reported feeling less depressed, and the parents noticed their interactions had improved. He seemed less irritated. Upon reflection, the parents agreed that the decreased isolation and increased structure, along with decreased electronic time, helped provide more support for the boy, as well as conveyed a message to him that his family wanted him to be more involved.

(Note: When implementing new interventions your child may appear frustrated. Here the goal was to connect more with child and decrease isolation, not make the child happy in the moment.)

Another Perspective on Communication

"My son and I had a tough time talking through our frustrations. **I realized that I tended to do a lot of lecturing, which created a greater distance between us.** *I started to lecture less and listen more while explaining to my son my feelings of frustration, and I modeled how to take a break when frustrated and come back to the conversation. My son started talking to me more about his feelings, which in turn improved our communication."*

~ Mary, mother of 2

I realized that I tended to do a lot of lecturing, which created a greater distance between us.

Traps

- Assuming something is wrong when we approach situations with our children, such as someone looks sad, and we say, "What is wrong?"

- Asking leading questions that may contain judgments, such as "Did you have anxiety today?" "Did you have someone to sit with at lunch?"

- Being hypervigilant to situations that may have been difficult for the child.

Avoid The Negative Trap

- Sometimes children live up to the reputation that has been created for them.

- The language we use reflects our focus. Words also create added meaning for the child and influences how they see themselves and their abilities.

- Look for opportunities to say, "Tell me something that went well today" or "Tell me about something that was difficult and how you worked through it."

- View overcoming adversity as a success, rather than focusing on the failure.

- Every day is a day where a lot happens. Avoid assigning judgment.

- Look for times when the child is solving his/her own difficulty and look for times when the child is behaving or making progress in an area.

- Avoid labeling the child. Not "You are anxious," or "You have issues with friends." Instead, share with your child that there are times when we all have issues in relationships.

Communicating Unspoken Expectations

If you look at your family, are there any unspoken expectations? Are there expectations that your children would say exist? These may be based on your responses, such as facial gestures, comments, and timing of responses. If you have ever thought, "They should know that is what I want," then you have an unspoken expectation. For instance, a mother continually asked her son about his grades, and when her son said that he got a B, she once said, "Was the assignment difficult?" The son's perspective was that the mother's response indicated that she expected higher than a B grade. This is an example of an unspoken expectation since the mother had not stated what grades she wanted. In addition, some unspoken expectations are based on the family dynamics and history. See the following example that may help you to understand better how this may happen without knowing it exists.

Example Case Study

A 16-year-old son stated that he needed to look for a job and would not attend college. The parents immediately started talking about how he could do anything, and the world is open to possibilities for him. The son interrupted the parents and said, "You did not go to college and neither did my sister." The son argued, "Everyone is successful." The parents agreed, but challenged the son on his dreams of being an engineer. The oldest daughter jumped into the discussion and identified she could relate to her brother. She said that she decided to attend cosmetology school and not attend the local community college because she could be successful without a degree and felt college, with her goals, was spending money foolishly. It was obvious that the parents were surprised by the children's conversations and feelings. Everyone agreed that college was encouraged in the home, but money was a concern and often a topic. As the conversation continued the entire family came to realize that an unspoken expectation existed within the family. This is neither a positive or negative belief, it is just a belief that existed in the home that was not directly discussed, although the children were aware of it through family interactions. From the parents' perspective, college was a given. From the children's perspective, there was the expectation of quicker career preparation.

Example Case Study

We met with an 8-year-old boy and his parents. This boy was struggling with performance anxiety. One thing we observed is that the mother and father told us a few times that this boy was gifted. It occurred to us that the boy knew of the label and interpreted the label to mean he needed to perform at a high level, which was feeding into the performance anxiety. We spent some time working with the parents, to shift from using terms like really bright and gifted, to help the child understand and embrace his strengths and weaknesses. This seemed to alleviate some of the anxiety and is an excellent representation of a growth mindset.

Another Perspective on Unspoken Expectations and Using a Growth Mindset

"I was making it a point to tell my daughter how talented she was on a regular basis. I wanted her to feel good about herself because she often became very self-critical. My counselor challenged me to tie praise or compliments to actions, rather than abstract approval not related to specifics, such as, "You are so wonderful or brilliant." Also, I started to discuss failures and mistakes and acknowledge positive ways she has dealt with those as well. This shift in my responses helped her gain more confidence, as well as to set more realistic expectations for herself."

~ Catherine, mother of 1

Reflective Questions

1. Are expectations spoken or unspoken in your home?

....
....
....
....

2. What are some unspoken expectations that your child may feel?

....
....
....
....

3. What are areas where your child can be self-critical?

....
....
....
....

A Solution-Focused Approach to Parenting

As therapists, we often take a solution-focused approach to parenting. We work with parents to help their children see their strengths and abilities. We want to make these strengths and skills more apparent to others in the child's life. This approach spends more time focusing on solutions and less time focusing on the problems. This approach stems from the conviction that people, especially children and adolescents, will feel more empowered by focusing on their strengths. Likewise, **children will feel more motivated to create solutions if they believe solutions are possible.**

*Children will feel more motivated to create solutions
if they believe solutions are possible.*

Example Case Study

We worked with a third-grade girl who felt like she could not manage her fears and was uncomfortable with handling new and difficult situations. We first noticed that she managed a few new situations during the past week. We further questioned her about how she was able to accomplish working through these difficult situations. We also spent some time recognizing that she seemed brave for handling situations that can cause her to be uncomfortable. We asked her about other new situations she had experienced and how she used bravery to work through those times, too. We compiled a list of bravery situations. We asked her what she thought would happen if she continued to take similar steps. She replied with a smile, "I am pretty brave." She thought the situations would become a little easier now that she noticed she could handle new situations.

It was important for this girl to recognize that she could and has handled new situations, even during times when she was uncomfortable. This was a shift in focus from spending a lot of time discussing her fears to recognizing her bravery.

Another Perspective on Language

"I found that I often asked my son if he was anxious prior to a situation that had caused him anxiety in the past. I realized my questioning about his anxiety was increasing his anxiety. I have learned to focus more on his healthy use of coping strategies, rather than questioning his anxiety. By doing so, I was really reacting to my own anxiety."

~ Bill, father of 2

I found that I often asked my son if he was anxious prior to a situation that had caused him anxiety in the past.

Sidetracking

Have you ever been part of a conversation that goes all over the place and when it ends, you do not understand what happened? Well, there is a good chance that sidetracking occurred. Sidetracking in communication occurs when individuals start responding to their internal experience and not to what is happening or being said. The use of sidetracking creates ineffective communication and may lead to more arguments.

Understanding your own emotions, and knowing how to respond effectively, will keep your conversation on track. This might be a good time to revisit your Obstacles to Effective Parenting Sheet. What emotions did you identify?

Understanding your own emotions, and knowing how to respond effectively, will keep your conversation on track.

Example Case Study

A father brings home flowers for his 15-year-old daughter. He knows that his daughter has been feeling down and thought the flowers would lift her spirits. She thanks him but does not seem as appreciative as he expected. He attempts to maintain a conversation but quickly finds himself frustrated, and then an argument begins. The father feels unappreciated and is reacting to his internal hurt, while the daughter feels as though no one quite understands her. She really appreciates the roses but feels her own father does not know that she prefers daisies to roses. The focus of the conversation moved to frustration, which led to a misunderstanding. It is not uncommon to see sidetracking in families because in family relationships we are more likely to respond out of emotions. It can quickly erode communication.

Reflective Question

1. What emotion or internal experience could be a potential opportunity for sidetracking?

....

....

....

....

Tips for More Purposeful Communication

- Provide the child with choices. Avoid saying things like, "You have to" or, "Yes you will" which can lead to power struggles. Look for opportunities to encourage growth by phrases such as, "It is your choice." Or, present two choices and give the results of each choice.

- Look for opportunities to respond with, "What do you think you could do?" or, "How could you handle this situation?" Evoke critical thinking skills by asking, "What are ways you have handled similar situations in the past?" versus reacting by providing solutions or attempting to fix the problem for the child.

- Recognize the words or phrases that place focus on certain areas and/or can reinforce certain beliefs and or viewpoints. Looking at questions or statements that are asked at the end of a school day, shift from asking about mistakes or shortcomings, or grades and achievement, and instead reinforce beliefs, such as compassion by asking about helping others.

- Avoid saying, "It will be a great day," if it may not be a great day. Instead, say, "It may be difficult, annoying, imperfect, tiring, etc., but what are some ways that you can manage?"

- Work on perspective and help the child to understand realistic viewpoints. Assist children in understanding other's points of view by explaining to them how you feel in certain situations, as well as asking prompting questions such as, "How do you think that made her/him feel when that happened?"

- Avoid over-reassurance and over-complimenting the child. These strategies do not raise confidence. Having more realistic conversations can set up the child to handle situations in a healthier way.

- Avoid negative talk about other parents, teachers and other key people in the child's life.

Reflective Questions

1. Does your use of language reflect your goals for your child? If so, how?

....
....
....
....

2. What is one area you would like to work on regarding your use of language?

....
....
....
....

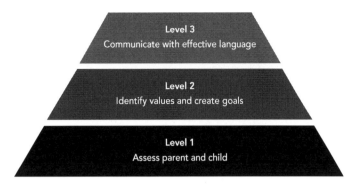

LEVEL 3 SUMMARY

What are the takeaways from Level 3, Communicate with Effective Language?

....
....
....
....
....
....
....
....
....
....
....
....
....
....
....
....
....
....
....
....
....
....
....
....
....
....
....

Write any questions or concerns you may want to explore more.

Chapter Five

LEVEL 4: DEAL WITH EMOTIONS: SELF AND CHILD

---

*The definition of insanity is continuing to do the same thing
but expecting a different result.*

~Unknown

It is Time to Do Something Different

When teaching parenting classes, we often use the iconic airplane analogy. If you are on an airplane, and the airplane experiences turbulence, you look to the flight attendant to assess the severity of the situation. If the flight attendant appears calm and does not show a distinct emotional reaction, passengers may assume that the situation is not severe. However, if the flight attendant shows an emotional reaction and quickly runs to each passenger attempting to soothe and reassure them, the passengers may experience heightened anxiety and assume that the situation is extreme.

As children grow and develop, they look to those around them to give meaning to different feelings and experiences. In fact, it is beneficial for a parent to normalize the child's experience of feelings, so he/she will learn to tolerate even the uncomfortable ones (Schwartz, 2015). When a child is experiencing distress, it is critical that the parents remain calm and refrain from excessive talking and reassurance. Calm relays a message the situation is manageable, and that fear, stress, and anxiety can be tolerated. The child will gain confidence and learn how to comfort him/herself when experiencing different emotions.

It is common for parents to feel uneasy and even feel sorry for their child when the child is experiencing discomfort. These feelings of uneasiness or guilt may influence the parenting responses to the child and result in parental responses being emotionally reactive rather than purposeful. Likewise, many parents attempt to relieve their own feelings by intervening and providing comfort and reassurance to their child, sometimes even solving or fixing the situation that created the distress. At times, if not dangerous, it is helpful for the parent to allow the child to experience some distress so that the child can learn to self-soothe and navigate through his/her situation, as well as future stressful experiences (Morin, 2017).

Parents who are more mindful of their own emotional reactions, and how their reactions manifest in their parenting, will have an increased understanding in terms of how these reactions impact their responses to their child. Parenting out of fear, guilt, or anger will not serve to teach the child lessons, but instead may cause more hurt feelings and resentments.

Reflective Questions

Return to your Obstacles to Effective Parenting Worksheet in Chapter 2.
Ask yourself these questions:

1. How do you respond when your child experiences distress?
   (*Sample answers: I feel guilty that I cannot give him/her enough. I become anxious, sad, worried, etc., and want to make him/her feel better.*)

   ....
   ....
   ....
   ....

2. Have you ever gotten into a power struggle with your child? Who won?
   (*Sample answers: No (LOL). No one.*)

   ....
   ....
   ....
   ....

3. What are times and topics in which you are more likely to engage in a power struggle with your child?
   (*Sample answers: When I am feeling a strong emotional reaction, such as guilt or anger.*)

   ....
   ....
   ....
   ....

4. What things trigger discomfort in your parenting?
   (*Sample answer: I become uncomfortable when my child is sad, hurt, anxious, etc.*)

   ....
   ....
   ....
   ....

5. How do you manage your emotional reactions when you are parenting?
   (*Sample answer: I like to take breaks and think about how the situation should resolve.*)

   ....
   ....
   ....
   ....

6. What types of situations make it difficult for you and increase your emotional reactivity?

   (*Sample answer: I am apprehensive when my child is struggling.*)

   ....

   ....

   ....

   ....

7. What are times you are more likely to react emotionally?

   (*Sample answer: When I become more upset, i.e., worried, exhausted, or tired from my work demands.*)

   ....

   ....

   ....

   ....

Something you may not know…

WE TEACH PEOPLE

TO **BE COMFORTABLE**

BEING UNCOMFORTABLE

A child can experience several feelings at one time but may hyper-focus on those feelings that are more undesirable. It is helpful for children to learn to sit with these feelings (Greenberg, 2017). **Although some feelings may seem more desirable, feelings are neither positive nor negative.** Instead, they are interpreted by each person differently. Most adults understand that feelings are not a permanent state of being. Feelings have a beginning, middle, and an end. A critical aspect of emotional health involves being able to recognize and experience different emotions, instead of striving to avoid certain ones, such as anxiety or sadness.

> *Although some feelings may seem more desirable,*
> *feelings are neither positive nor negative.*

Most people experience some sort of anxiety (discomfort) daily. We often use the term discomfort rather than anxiety. We find that the term anxiety tends to be overused, as opposed to normalizing a child's experience of different feelings. In fact, research shows that it is important for us to learn to face our fears and practice experiencing discomfort. To sit with feelings of discomfort, one will need to be able to self-soothe and tolerate the uncomfortable.

A child's emotional functioning can be impacted by heightened anxiety, as well as other psychiatric conditions. It is important to help children to recognize that they can label and tolerate their feelings. Feelings do have different intensity levels at varying points but do pass with time. We try not to assign positive or negative labels to feelings, even though some feelings may be more pleasurable versus uncomfortable. This helps with teaching the child how to manage and tolerate different feelings and emotions.

Reflective Question

1. Ask yourself when you are responding to your child: is my reaction coming from my own emotional response, or from the goals I have set for my parenting?

....

....

....

....

Get comfortable being uncomfortable.
Get confident being uncertain.
Do not give up just because something is hard.
Pushing through challenges is what makes us grow.

Unknown

Below is The Growth Zones Chart. Jack J. Lesyk, Ph.D., CMPC from the Ohio Center for Sport Psychology and the sport psychologist for the Cleveland Cavilers, often references this chart when discussing growth and opportunities. We often use the chart to discuss the importance of allowing children opportunities to experience some discomfort and move out of their comfort zone to experience growth. We may feel more at ease when our children are comfortable, but it will be times they come out of their comfort zone, and do things that are difficult for them, that will allow them to grow. The high-risk zone represents an area in which you take more risks, success may be greater but less frequent, and there is a higher opportunity for failure. When in the high-risk zone it is important to have realistic expectations, and awareness of limitations and obstacles. Assessing a child's level of skill and emotional development, as well as creating realistic expectations based on strengths and weaknesses, will assist the child in reaching his/her potential and growth.

Comfort Zone	Growth Zone	High Risk Zone

Difficulty

We have seen that children gain confidence in their abilities when they inch out of their comfort zone, take on new challenges, and accomplish tasks that are new or were difficult. This does not mean overloading oneself, but rather moving out of the comfort zone. Self-esteem and self-respect stem from a belief that one is competent, which is strengthened as one learns he/she is capable based on working through new challenges. Confidence occurs even when the child does not reach success on the attempted task; the mere attempt is building confidence.

According to Dr. Nathaniel Branden (Branden, 1994), "Self-esteem is the disposition to experience oneself as being competent to cope with the basic challenges of life, and as being worthy of happiness. Thus, it consists of two components: (1) self-efficacy – confidence in one's ability to think, learn, choose, and make appropriate decisions; and (2) self-respect – confidence that love, friendship, achievement, success – in a word, happiness – are natural and appropriate."

When we first read Dr. Branden's passage, we knew we had to support our clients in building confidence, but also in embracing the belief that they were worthy of being loved, finding success, and experiencing happiness.

Some of our work has also been influenced by Carol Dweck, Ph.D. and her theory of the Growth Mindset (Dweck, 2016). **When we look at children, we understand that as they learn to tolerate discomfort, they grow and gain confidence that they can face challenges that lie ahead.** Many of the children we work with who have stayed stagnant in the comfort zone, often struggle with the belief that they cannot manage, which in turn can lower their confidence and create feelings of inadequacy. Confidence comes from enduring challenges and recognizing steps taken.

When we look at children, we understand that as they learn to tolerate discomfort, they grow and gain confidence that they can face challenges that lie ahead.

Most children overcome challenges every day. Below is a strategy we use that helps the child to build self-reliance and manage situations.

Create a Success Journal or Solution Notebook

We suggest you have your child record a challenge he/she faces each day, along with the ways he/she can manage and create a solution. When the child runs into a difficult situation, cue the child to read the journal and reflect on strategies, as well as to look back to see if he/she has dealt with similar issues in the past.

Children Who "Fall Apart" More at Home

Sometimes, children arrive home and decompensate or have trouble managing emotions. They cry and melt down. It can be easy to justify these behaviors by explaining this is a form of stress release and acceptable because they are more comfortable within the home environment. However, it is vital to encourage and expect healthy methods of stress management. Children who are exhibiting maladaptive coping strategies, such as melting down, isolating, or becoming excessively emotional, may need increased structure. Structure may mean having a routine for after school, especially regarding expectations around homework, dinner, and bedtime routines. When there are immature or unhealthy methods of coping, evaluate how you are responding to those responses.

Do not reinforce behavior you do not want to see.

Many parents find that expectations and structure help to increase confidence by allowing the child to experience success when meeting expectations and navigating structure.

Parents should not engage when a child is using ineffective communication skills and non-age-appropriate behaviors (i.e., a teen crying and screaming), but rather cue the child to take some time and resume communication when he/she has calmed down. For example, "It seems as though you are upset. Why don't we take a break and use some of your calming strategies, and we can come back to this conversation in few moments?" It is important to return to the conversation once the child has calmed down.

(Note: this may be a wise time to reflect on your parenting goals. If your goal is to increase healthy coping management, cueing the child to utilize healthier coping may be a strategy to reflect that goal).

Allowing inappropriate behavior fosters emotional immaturity. Likewise, this strategy can be used, if as a parent, you are feeling emotional. This will be an excellent opportunity to model to your child that you recognize you are getting emotional and taking a break.

Allowing inappropriate behavior fosters emotional immaturity.

Reflective Questions

1. What are some ways your child manages stress and feelings of discomfort?
   (*Sample answer: My child cries and becomes inconsolable.*)

....

....

....

....

2. What types of situations cause your child to feel uncomfortable?
   (*Sample answer: When my child perceives unfair treatment.*)

....

....

....

....

3. How do you respond when your child begins to experience discomfort?
   (*Sample answer: I start talking to offer solutions and help my child to recognize other perspectives.*)

....

....

....

....

Do not worry that children never listen to you;
worry that they are always watching you.

Robert Fulghum (Zimmer, 2003)

Texting Your Child When They Are at School

Parents can explain and model for their children how to manage stress and discomfort, especially how to access supports when at school or even other locations. If you recognize you frequently text your child to check in and/or see if they are ok, reflect on the purpose of the texts. Specifically, try to recognize if they are a result of your parenting goal or if they could be due to an emotional reaction. Similarly, if your child is frequently texting you from school for reassurance, encourage your child to use their school supports. If your child does not know the supports at school and how to access them (i.e., a nurse for a headache or counselor if feeling sad), this will be a great opportunity to review them with your child.

If the texting continues, explain that your goal is for them to learn to access school supports and that you will not respond to texts during school hours. If you are concerned about your child while they are at school, consult with your child's school teacher and/or other school staff. Parents have often told us that their children are seeking reassurance when texting from school. While it may be anxiety provoking to receive these texts, keep in mind that reassurance seeking can heighten and prolong anxiety. We have found that this exercise has helped create greater self-reliance and confidence for the child, especially the child exhibiting symptoms of anxiety, as he/she learns to work through their discomfort and seek appropriate supports when needed.

Reflective Questions

1. How do you personally manage stress and feelings of discomfort?

....
....
....
....

2. Who are other support people in your child's life?

....
....
....
....

3. How can you encourage your child to use his/her supports?

....
....
....
....

4. How often do you text your child to check in, or check in on them through other avenues?

....
....
....
....

There are various recommended coping strategies out there today, all from different schools of thought. We work with our parents and children to focus on strategies that encourage them to be present in the moment, increase self-awareness, and better manage an emotional experience. In turn, by allowing the child to experience opportunities rather than engage in avoidance and reassurance-seeking during stressful times, and by balancing emotions and judgments, this will help to calm the child's frame of mind.

*Sometimes we remind our families that
the only constant is change.*

Healthy Coping Strategies

1. Breathing techniques

   a. Color breathing: breathe in a color that you find pleasing. Breathe out a color that is not as pleasing

   b. Triangle breathing: breathe in for two seconds, hold for two seconds and breathe out for two seconds

2. Facts versus judgments

   a. Recording the facts and judgments of the situation, recognizing how the judgments impact views.

3. Reframing thoughts, recognizing distorted thought patterns. Listen to your thoughts and notice negative patterns, such as, "I am not good enough". Next identify some common negative thoughts you experience and come up with ways to reframe those thoughts. When you notice one of the negative thoughts, acknowledge, challenge the thought with truths, and then replace with the reframe.

4. Grounding techniques. These are techniques that involve being fully present in your body and/or mind. Feeling connected to the earth, by bringing your mind and body to the present moment. One activity that we suggest is checking in with your five senses, such as taking a moment to observe what you see, hear, touch, smell and taste. This exercise can allow the person a chance to enter a state of calm momentarily.

5. Mindfulness techniques. The goal of these techniques is to assist one in achieving an alert focused state of relaxation by deliberately paying attention to thoughts and sensations without judgment. All mindfulness techniques are a form of meditation. One example is sitting down and taking a moment to pause, by observing thoughts and watching them pass, as one continually refocuses attention to the present. Another example is taking a moment to observe one's surroundings while taking a mental note of each external item in the environment.

6. Sleep hygiene
   a. Getting enough sleep, limiting electronics prior to bedtime

7. Nutrition
   a. Healthy well-balanced meals and snacks

8. Art or music

9. Taking a pause to just to be for a few moments

LEVEL 4 SUMMARY

What are the takeaways from Level 4, Dealing with Emotions (Self and Child)?

Write any questions or concerns you may want to explore more.

Chapter Six

LEVEL 5: CREATE YOUR PLAN

Where are we going? One day Alice came to a fork in the road and saw a Cheshire cat in a tree. "Which road do I take?" she asked. "Where do you want to go?" was his response. "I do not know," Alice answered. "Then," said the cat, "it does not matter."

Lewis Carroll, Alice in Wonderland (Carroll, 2016)

We often think about the saying, "If you do not have a plan for how to get there, how do you know where you are going?"

Why a Plan?

Most parents we work with will agree that plans are good. Go to the basics to start. Since we know that part of childhood development includes testing limits and challenging the environment, which can lead to frustration for most of us, we have found parents find comfort in having a plan, especially a plan for response during challenging times. It is sometimes through these challenging times that children begin to understand right and wrong, to learn to take responsibility, and ideally start to create self-discipline. **Challenges are advantageous!** The key is how you respond, even more importantly than the problem itself, at times.

Challenges are advantageous!

Having a plan assists parents in developing and recognizing responses that will guide the child to successfully self-navigate.

The level of structure and plan will look different in every household. It is helpful to create a plan that fits your parenting style and the needs of your family. Please avoid the one size fits all approach to building a plan. Make the plan *your* plan. In our experience, children of all ages thrive within a more structured setting that entails consistency and a program.

The Center for Disease Control (CDC) website *https://www.cdc.gov/parents/essentials/structure/index.html* has a lot of useful worksheets and information. It is an excellent resource for parents. Below is just a snippet from the website:

Three key ingredients to building structure in the home:

Consistency – doing the same thing every time

Predictability – expecting or knowing what is going to happen

Follow-through – enforcing the consequence

Structure ~ Find Your Balance, Align Your Plan

An easy way to think of structure is order or routine.

Often, plans mean direction, routine, and identifying some goal points. A benefit will be some added structure to your household.

Think for a moment about what the term structure means to you. Structure can look different in every household. When we discuss structure, it is not intended to be overwhelming, but rather to simplify daily life. Find your balance when devising your plan. Balance includes deciding what is important, realistic, and attainable for your household.

For some, a comprehensive plan will be helpful, and for others, adding elements will be more realistic. For instance, in one family, the mother and father developed some structure by establishing a bedtime routine for their children. If they were ready for bed, meaning teeth brushed and in their pajamas by 8:00 p.m., the children earned an extra 15 minutes of story time with their parents. This was one way that the family implemented some structure and over time developed a routine. In creating this evening routine, the family noticed how it also helped shape the rest of the evening to be a more positive experience for all.

We are excited to come alongside you and help you create your own personalized family plan. The family plan will help implement some routine within the home, as well as provide a sense of comfort for the family members that a plan simply exists. We have found that structure and well-thought-out plans assist the parents in reducing their emotional reactivity.

We use this analogy for our parents. Think about a young child and how limits are created for outdoor play. Children are not left to roam wherever they desire. Set parameters and identified boundaries clearly define where the child may play or go. The child has free choice on where or what they play within limits. We would all agree a three-year-old would not be permitted to play on the front lawn without supervision. Setting limits ensures safety and promotes emotional growth. It is important that boundaries are clear and realistic for the child. Unrealistic expectations will create frustration, anger, and power struggles, just like if the three-year-old was allowed to play out front alone but was told not to leave the yard.

We recommend you review your family's plan regularly with your child. This does not need to mean long drawn out conversations, but merely having some time set aside each week to review the basics of the plan, and some key highlights, such as goals, expectations, or progress (discussed further in the next section). Many parents find that reviewing the plan weekly can be helpful in maintaining the plan and open dialogue.

When creating the plan, it will be important to take into consideration the child's goals. The parent(s) are still creating the plan, but acknowledging the child's input, such as asking questions like, "What are some of your goals?" or "What do you think are realistic expectations and privileges?" will help the child to "buy-in" to the plan and keep the child connected. These questions will need to be adapted depending on the child's age and level of emotional functioning.

For instance, your adolescent says he/she wants you off his/her back and you want your child to be more independent. So, both you and your child are seeking the same outcome goal. Recognize that similarity can open the door for a conversation about ways to meet goals. If you and your child do not agree on the outcome goal, maybe incorporate some aspects of your child's ideas and then explain how they may be further incorporated as the plan goes on. Remember change can be difficult, and if this is a new approach in your home, your child may resist.

Consider the child who wants more privileges and independence. When creating and reviewing plans, encourage the child to identify ways to be more independent. While parents will most often need to have the final say in determining if the goals, expectations, and privileges are realistic and healthy, hearing and taking the child's input into account is key. Once the plan is established, avoiding power struggles and negotiations around expectations will be important. Reserve discussion for those regular meeting times unless it cannot be avoided. Sometimes, families with multiple children in their household will have one child who is demonstrating more concerning behaviors. We recommended including all children in the plan. Family plans have been found to promote uniformity in the household, as well as avoiding further isolation of one child.

The reality is, as adults, we have many responsibilities. Remember, there are ways to implement a simple structure with routine and consistency even amongst these many responsibilities.

The End Result of a Lack of Consistency May Be…

All of us can relate to having responsibilities inside or outside of the home. When we do not perform expected work tasks, we face the consequences. If we work outside of the home, the boss may not excuse or diminish expectations because we are tired, anxious, or have a headache or stomach ache. Often, as adults, we do not have a day off or a break; the expectations and demands are always there and we must meet them. When the consequences are clearly understood and reinforced, we are more motivated to meet expectations.

It would be difficult to work in a setting in which the boss is continually altering expectations, as well as sending mixed messages. An example might be when a boss is angry one day for tardiness, but the next day excuses the tardiness, saying it is all right or makes a joke about the situation. The lack of consistency increases anxiety and frustration. Therefore, we encourage and promote establishing clear and consistent expectations with all children in the home.

Creating Goals Will Be the Foundation of the Plan

At this time, think about some of the goals that you want your parenting to reflect. Again, be clear about **What Type of Adult Are You Trying to Raise?** What are some of those characteristics you want your adult child to have? What are some goals you have for your child? As we mentioned earlier, we will refer to outcome goals when creating the plan, because we encourage you to focus on the outcome you are trying to achieve. Some examples of outcome goals are greater self-reliance, more independence, increased self-confidence, and better problem-solving skills.

What type of adult are you trying to raise?

Reflective Questions

1. List three to five outcome goals that you would like to reflect your parenting. (Look back at the goals you previously created, has anything changed?)

....

....

....

....

....

....

2. What are some outcome goals that your child has for him/herself?

....

....

....

....

....

....

Expectations

Creating and defining outcome goals will help you to develop expectations and privileges which will provide your child a better understanding of the logic behind the expectations. You will notice that we tend to use the term 'earning privileges' as opposed to 'consequences.' This is because we have found that privileges help to motivate the child.

Refer to the Emotional Development Scale from Level 1 for help creating goals and, setting expectations, as well as monitoring development. Below are some reflective questions so you can examine your current way of doing things. Remember please, avoid self-criticism or assigning blame to the other parent in this exercise. Just identify how things are going in the household currently.

Reflective Questions

1. What are the expectations you currently have for your child? (How do you respond currently if those expectations are not met?)

....

....

....

....

2. How do you feel if those expectations are not met, and what are the emotional responses you demonstrate when they are not achieved (frustrated, angry, etc.)?

....

....

....

....

3. Is your child aware of how you will respond if the expectations are not met?

....

....

....

....

4. Would your child/children say that you are consistent with follow through on the expectations?

....

....

....

....

5. What would your child say are some realistic expectations?

....

....

....

....

The Process-Mindset

We have discovered that parents find more success and less frustration when working from the process-mindset framework. We really, really, do not want you to skip this step. It is an essential aspect to creating and monitoring expectations.

The process-mindset is the method of staying grounded in the moment and focusing on the current expectations versus focusing on the outcome goals. The process-mindset allows a parent to identify obstacles and ways to problem solve obstacles, and this naturally creates a flow for follow through. Parents will strengthen the plan by working to create realistic expectations. It is important to avoid evaluating the achievement of the outcome goals daily. This might be a different way of thinking for you. We encourage the parent and child to stay in the process-mindset as much as possible. This will be important when it comes to creating and implementing your plan. Recognize that as the child starts to meet the expectations, the child's actions (and decisions) align with the parenting goal.

Creating Expectations

Expectations should be reasonable and focused on targeting key behaviors, as well as derived from the parenting goals and values. **When creating expectations for a child, it will be helpful to keep the expectations aligned with the child's current emotional level of development.** This will help the child's maturation. Expectations set too high or too low could negatively impact the child's emotional growth and functioning. The child may feel a sense of despair or failure if unable to meet expectations that are too high, or not push him/herself to thrive if expectations are too low. Many parents will say that recognizing realistic expectations can be tricky, especially if the child has emotional or medical concerns.

When creating expectations for a child, it will be helpful to keep the expectations aligned with the child's current emotional level of development.

It is vital for children to learn to recognize and appreciate both their strengths and weaknesses, as well as to hold realistic expectations regarding their own performance. Throughout this process, we encourage parents to help their children recognize and openly discuss these areas, so that the children can be in a better place to create healthy expectations for themselves. Many children will say that they feel better when they realize that they do not have to always have 'perfect' performance. Moreover, parents understanding these strengths and weaknesses will be more effective at setting goals, establishing expectations, and implementing the plan.

Recognizing the difference between rules and expectations creates consistency and aligns with the growth mindset approach. Remember, expectations for family members are based on defined goals. Each family member works toward meeting the expectations to help the family unit create harmony and exist within the stated or agreed upon values. Avoid setting expectations out of emotion and avoid punitive consequences and rules that may feel rigid to the child. Making blanket threats diminishes the parent's place in the family unit. Only say what can and will be followed.

To stay in a process mindset, the focus should be on the expectations. We have found this enhances the parent's ability to respond to his/her child in the moment. For instance, a goal may be to teach the child that he or she can manage discomfort, thus promoting confidence in handling stressful situations and a greater sense of independence. Using this goal as an example, a parent may choose to not engage with and react to an adolescent who is experiencing discomfort, but instead, allow the adolescent to work through the discomfort.

Conversely, an emotionally charged reaction may involve a parent rushing in to relieve the child's distress, thus sending a message to the child that he or she cannot work through the discomfort on their own. We can all recognize times that we have parented primarily out of emotion, which can lead to inconsistent parenting, as well as emotionally charged responses.

Parents are encouraged to write expectations out for their children and review weekly with the children, along with the goals and overall plan. These are those meetings we referred to in the goal section. Remember, during the review time, you might find it helpful to discuss progress, obstacles, and ways to problem solve. The plan will be further strengthened by having these meetings, which will help to develop consistency and a routine. While children may give feedback during the weekly meetings, avoid power struggles and negotiations with the child regarding the expectations once they are set.

Here are some examples of outcome goals and expectations that parents have used during their work with us. These are only examples and may not reflect your goals. These are just guides. If you want to refresh your memory on the definition of goals, go to the GLOSSARY. Perhaps refresh your understanding by rereading your answers in Level #2.

Examples of Outcome Goals and Expectations for Children (Birth to age 12) and Adolescents (ages 12 – 18)

Outcome Goal: Greater Self-Reliance

    Expectation Child: Be able to ask a teacher for help.

    Expectation Adolescent: Purchase gas when the tank is ¼ full.

Outcome Goal: More Independence

    Expectation Child: The child will be able to brush teeth.

    Expectation Adolescent: The adolescent will be able to get him/herself up and ready for school.

Outcome Goal: Increased Self Confidence

    Expectation Child: Identify one strength or recognize something that the child is proud of.

    Expectation Adolescent: Identify 3-5 strengths.

Outcome Goal: Better Problem-Solving Skills

    Expectation Child: The child will be able to improvise and substitute a missing piece to a game.

    Expectation Adolescent: The adolescent will be able to speak with a teacher if he/she is feeling overwhelmed with a project or task.

Create Your Own Parenting Outcome Goals and Expectations for Your Child

Outcome Goal:

....
....
....
....
....

Expectation:

....
....
....
....
....

Outcome Goal:

....
....
....
....
....

Expectation:

....
....
....
....
....

Outcome Goal:

....
....
....
....
....

Expectation:

....
....
....
....
....

Privileges and Motivation

Think about times where it may be difficult to work towards the goal. For instance, someone may write, "I want my teenage son to be more independent, but I recognize if I do not wake him up for school, he'll be late." In this example, the outcome goal is for the adolescent to be more independent, and the expectation is for the adolescent to wake himself up for school. If the parent decides that he/she is not going to wake up the adolescent for school, it will be important for school consequences to occur. Too often, parents set expectations and give threats, but struggle following though. Expectations will be maintained by follow through. To reinforce a goal, you can create more than one expectation for each goal. Providing differing privileges for meeting expectations can also help motivate the child and shift concerning behaviors.

In our experience, privileges can be used as motivators and given only when the child has met expectations. This will allow for a greater understanding of the expectations, as well as help to motivate the child to meet expectations and even work through feelings of distress. Also, via parenting strategies, the child will be able to learn to be more responsible, which should carry over to other settings, such as school or work.

According to this line of thought, privileges are identified to coordinate with certain expectations met. For instance, if the child is ready for school on time, a child may earn 30 minutes of screen time or electronics time. These privileges will help motivate the child to meet expectations, as well as teach responsibility. Again, if you do not attend work, you will not get paid.

Does your child view privileges as rights? Electronics, social engagements, cars, toys, etc., may be seen by many as rights. When creating the new family plan, we will challenge you to think about such things as privileges.

To develop consistency, some parents find it beneficial to write out expectations and privileges to establish a better routine. Review these guidelines weekly to ensure consistency and discuss progress at that point. Discuss obstacles and ways to problem-solve the barriers. Be aware of the strategies that will support implementation, as well as aid in success. Some of these strategies include avoiding excessive talking, negotiating, and altering expectations due to 'feeling sorry' for the child.

One parent told us that she continually gave her son the privilege of video games even though he did not earn the time because she felt bad for him and worried that the video games were the only thing that made him happy. Providing the child a privilege without meeting the expectation will further reinforce the problem behavior or avoidance.

Caution: Avoid engaging if your child is not using appropriate communication skills and age-appropriate behaviors, i.e., a teen crying and screaming. Cue the child to take some time and resume communication when he or she has calmed down. *In most cases, the child/adolescent has a choice in how he or she manages his or her emotions. Allowing inappropriate behaviors continues to foster emotional immaturity.*

Caution: Avoid engaging if your child is not using appropriate communication skills and age-appropriate behaviors.

For instance, a mother was speaking to her 10-year-old daughter, and the daughter raised her voice. The mother sensed the daughter was feeling overwhelmed; the mother said, "You look like you are getting upset. Yelling will not be helpful for either one of us, so take a few minutes to calm yourself, and we can return to this conversation once you are calm." If the child did not calm herself down, the mother was going to provide the child with some options, such as reminding the child of the expectation and privilege that was reflected in their plan. The privilege, in this case, was extra time with friends that day *(the privilege will be chosen based on what motivates the child)*. When creating the plan, you will be guided to align the privilege to the needs of the individual child, based on age and emotional functioning. This is also an example of a time in which having the plan was helpful. The child was able to calm down because the mother had consistently used this strategy for a few weeks.

Some parents have concerns over limiting electronic time or social time due to fear the child will become sad or make threats. In some cases, threats or verbal or physical aggression can occur. If this is the case, it will be essential to have an idea/plan ahead of time of how you will handle it. We will discuss this in further detail in the upcoming section.

Reflective Questions

1. What are privileges that your child has?

....

....

....

....

2. What types of privileges motivate your child?

....

....

....

....

3. Can you identify times when your child has surprised you by easily meeting an expectation that has been difficult in the past?

....

....

....

....

4. Identify a time that your child has been inconsistent in meeting his/her expectations. Are the motivators different? Do you notice a pattern?

....

....

....

....

5. How does your child respond to limited privileges?

....

....

....

....

6. Can you identify IN ADVANCE when you will be tempted to "give in"?

....

....

....

....

7. What will be some obstacles in implementing this plan?

....

....

....

....

8. How will you manage if your child is upset with you?

....

....

....

....

Plans do not have to be complex and difficult to follow. Create one that is realistic and works for your family. Below is one sample plan that a family used.

Sample Family Plan

Outcome Goal: Be more responsible and better decision making

Expectations	Privileges
Safe Choices	Decreased Supervision
Attend School	2 Hours of Screen Time
Be Ready & On Time for School	Social Time at Night
Chores/Responsibilities	Allowance
Homework	Cell Phone Privilege

Safety Concerns

If there are any safety concerns with the child, such as suicidal ideation, self-harm behaviors, poor nutrition, or verbal and physical aggression, these can be targeted first under the expectation section. If these should occur, take clearly defined next steps. Depending on the age of the child and cognitive level/emotional level, it is appropriate to say that you will contact law enforcement or seek mental health evaluation if you or another member feel unsafe. Feeling unsafe can mean feeling fear of threats of violence or intimidation, as well as concern for safety to self. Law enforcement or emergency assistance should be explained as support and assistance that would only be sought if safety concerns arose to help protect the child or family member. It is crucial that safety concerns are clearly stated, and in what type of situations a call will be made to involve assistance from law enforcement.

If you have defined the situations when a call will be made, you will need to follow through and make the call. We have found that children get confused when mixed messages occur, which increases their anxiety and may even elicit anger. If there are concerns that a child or adolescent self-harms, becomes physically aggressive, runs away, or threatens to harm him/herself in any way, your child must know what will happen. Below are examples of statements that parents have said to their children when there were concerns about immediate risk of harm or safety.

Child: "If you run away or try to hurt yourself or us, we need to call emergency assistance to help us."

Adolescent: "If we are concerned that you are not able to keep yourself safe, we will have to take you in for a mental health evaluation. If your behavior is escalating, and we are concerned that you are becoming physically aggressive, we will have to call 911 for assistance, to ensure your safety and ours."

Do not go it alone. Get help if you are concerned about your child's safety or potential to harm self or others!

When discussing these concerns with the child, focus on the message that safety and managing emotional and behavioral responses are expectations for health and wellness. If safety is a concern, the result may be an increase in supervision, such as the bedroom door being removed, no electronics without supervision, or being monitored until safety concerns have subsided.

(Note: Again, if there are concerns about the immediate risk of harm, please contact 911 or go to your local emergency room. Verbal or physical aggression, also a safety concern, can also result in the need to call 911. These possible consequences should be explained to the child when reviewing expectations and the plan.)

It is important to review healthy coping strategies with the child and use language that reflects that they have some choices regarding how they manage. Here is an example that a parent shared with us. The parent told the child, "I will respond based on how you are functioning. If you choose to become physically aggressive, we call the police." Try to remain calm when discussing serious safety expectations, and we cannot over-emphasize follow through. If you identify to the child your planned response, it is vital that you follow through. Empty threats will lead to more chaos.

Sometimes with extreme behaviors, reactions may need to be bold, primarily to establish an appropriate scope of authority. It will be important to have a clear understanding of how these behaviors will be handled, especially if there is an escalation of these behaviors when the plan is first being implemented.

Example Case Study

We worked with a 13-year-old girl engaging in self-harm behaviors. She reported that she only felt triggered to self-harm at home and felt better when she went out with her friends. The parent said that one of her parenting goals was to encourage distress tolerance and to help her daughter learn healthier ways to manage when she was upset. The mom explained to her daughter the goals. The mom set an expectation of safety and managing using healthier coping strategies, which included communicating with mom when she was having upset feelings or urges to engage in self-harm behaviors.

The mother further explained that because of concerns for her safety she would have to keep the bedroom door open at night and the daughter would receive more supervision when with friends and on electronics. The child became upset and said that she felt that was unfair and that she was being punished for her emotional issues. The mom explained that increased structure had been recommended to provide additional support. While the daughter was frustrated with the structure initially, she benefited from the consistency and was more motivated to work on healthy coping strategies to earn her privilege of more freedom and less supervision. As shown here, responding in a way that places the child more accountable for their choices and helps motivate them for the healthier option puts them in the driver seat of their outcomes. We call it meeting the child where he/she is at and encouraging healthy growth.

Reflective Question

1. Identify any safety concerns that you have for your child.

....

....

....

....

WHAT IS YOUR PLAN?

Below we give some examples of some expectations that have been created based on outcome goals. It is a little different from the last section as we list the privileges as well as obstacles. Next, you will find a template to create your plan. Use the following examples as a guide. Your plan does not have to be long-winded or overly detailed. After each goal, list the expectations for your child. It is important to note the obstacles that may occur in setting and following through with the expectations. Next, decide what privileges will be given for each expectation met, and/or loss of a privilege if the expectation is not met. It will be important for the child/adolescent to have some buy-in regarding the plan. During the development of the plan, children may have input into the privilege section with the parents' guidance. It will be important that they are realistic. Recognizing the obstacles will help you be better prepared for those challenges that may arise.

These are some examples parents have created as part of their plan.

Outcome Goal: Increase Anger Management Skills

Expectation Child: Identify emotion of anger and the secondary emotion. An example, a child is hurt and responds with anger. Help the child to identify that the child is hurt, and he/she reacted with anger in the situation.

Expectation Adolescent: Demonstrate containment of emotional outburst by verbalizing the experience to supports and when it is appropriate to do so.

Privilege (What will motivate your child/the buy-in): The child can choose a fun activity (child); earn more electronic time (adolescent).

Obstacles a parent may experience to hold the expectation: The parent may struggle to manage anger when the child becomes defiant.

Outcome Goal: Safety - Make Healthier Decisions

Expectation Child: The child will not engage in self-harm behaviors (banging head, cutting, etc.).

Expectation Adolescent: The adolescent will not engage in self-destructive behaviors (self-injury, substance use behaviors).

Privilege (What will motivate your child/the buy-in): The child will have more unsupervised time if the child demonstrates he/she can manage emotions (possibly time alone in a room, door closed, unsupervised time on electronics.) With a younger child, explain how the parent will respond during these instances.

Obstacles a parent may experience to hold the expectation: The parent feels guilty and fearful of these behaviors.

Now that you have established your goals, laid out your expectations, and identified privileges, create your Family Plan. Throughout this process, look for opportunities that allow the child to make choices and be accountable for decisions. For instance, provide the child with expectations, and make sure they know what will occur if they do not meet expectations. In this example, the child will be able to make an informed decision as to whether they are going to meet the expectation or not, and if they are willing to endure the consequence.

Some parents identify the most challenging part of the process is allowing the child to have choice.

(Note: If you struggle seeing your child making decisions that will have negative consequences, you may interrupt the process and attempt to redirect the child. We encourage parents to avoid enabling the child unless safety is a concern. We have found these opportunities promote growth in critical thinking skills, and children learn how to make decisions based on outcomes.)

Our Family Plan

Post this list somewhere you will see it. These goals will help you keep your responses and expectations inline and decrease emotional reactivity.

Note: Plans do not have to be complex and difficult to follow. Create one that is realistic and works for your family.

Outcome Goals:

1.
2.
3.
4.
5.

Expectations:

1.
2.
3.
4.
5.

Privileges (What will motivate your child/the "buy-in"):

1.
2.
3.
4.
5.

Obstacles a parent may experience to hold the expectation:

1.
2.
3.
4.
5.

Another Perspective on Creating a Plan

"When I started to be more consistent with my expectations and responses, I found that it caused less conflict between my son and myself. Also, his behavioral outbursts decreased, as I was more consistent with the ways I responded to his behaviors."

~John, father of 2

It is especially imperative for children with undesirable or non-age-appropriate behaviors to have structure in their home settings, even though they will probably resist it at first. Over time, the consistency will create a sense of safety and serve to decrease the behaviors. If you have concerns about these behaviors as mentioned earlier, it is recommended to seek a consult and professional assistance.

Challenges

It can be challenging to set limits. Most parents will say that it is difficult for them to see a child upset, although focusing on the goals with the child can increase understanding. The parent(s) is encouraged to reflect on his or her strengths and weaknesses, as well as the parenting goals during this time. Some parents will also discuss how formulating this plan can be difficult as it may upset the child. The goal is to promote emotional health and growth. The most natural word a parent can say to their child is "Yes," but setting boundaries with the child will lead to emotional growth long-term, despite that the child may experience being upset in the moment.

When first implementing the plan, it may cause increased resistance from the child, mainly since this may be a shift in your parenting. Expect some pushback. It will take a few weeks of consistency to establish a routine.

Example Case Study

An expectation for a 16-year-old adolescent may be to wake up with an alarm on time for school. Help the child to understand that meeting expectations will earn certain privileges and create independence. The child will earn privileges if the expectation is met, even if emotional or somatic reasons interfered with the child meeting expectations. The expectation is to wake up with the alarm even if they are feeling tired or anxious. The goal is not to punish a child for not feeling well, but rather to create structure and increase the child's emotional maturity.

Another Perspective on Creating a Plan

I would get frustrated and go into my teenage daughter's room several times each morning to try to get her to wake up for school. I found myself on some mornings yelling and threatening to take away privileges if she did not get up. I realized I was just becoming more frustrated and not helping the situation. We had discussed ways to help her increase responsibility, so I was only going to wake her up one time. Together we created a transition plan for the next month. If she did not wake up, she would have limited phone access that day. Plus, the consequence from the school, if she arrives late to school, is detention. After a few weeks, she started to get up on her own to her alarm. We definitely had our moments but keeping focused on our progress allowed me not to feel so frustrated on days things did not work as I hoped."

~Jenny, mother of 3

Reflective Questions

Look at the Obstacles to Effective Parenting Worksheet in Chapter 2.

1. What behaviors cause you to react emotionally?

....

....

....

....

2. Can you add more to your list now?

....

....

....

....

3. What are times that your child can manage difficult situations appropriately?

....

....

....

....

4. Can you list an area or two where you would like to increase your child's emotional functioning?

a. ....

....

....

....

b. ....

....

....

....

Avoid self-criticism and judgment when creating and following through. This is not about perfection. You are aiming for progress, improvement, growth, and consistency.

Avoid making excuses for all inappropriate behaviors. Recognizing behavior patterns is essential, but there is not always a need to understand root causes or diagnose every action.

When the Co-Parent Does Not Agree or Is Absent

If there are two parents in a child's life, whether in the same household or not, it is best for the parents to have expectations that are aligned. However, this may not be possible or realistic. In these instances, try to reinforce to the child that both parents have the same goal and mission (to support the child, etc.), even if the parents differ on approach and implementation.

At the end of the day, the most overwhelming key to a child's success is the positive involvement of the parents.

Jane D. Hull (as cited in Culp, 2018)

What if You Cannot Provide Unified Co-Parenting?

There are going to be circumstances in which you are not able to align with the other parent, or you may be in a situation in which there is not another co-parent. Do not despair! Remind yourself that you can only be the best parent that you can be, and THAT IS ENOUGH! Every family is different, and it is essential to work with the resources that you have.

If you find yourself in a single parent situation, where you do not have the support of the other parent, you may want to seek outside supports and resources to help guide and support you on this journey. Some of these supports may be available within the extended family, friends, neighbors, local churches, and community organizations. As difficult as it may be, it is important to ask for help. We all need it from time to time, and a support network could not be any more critical than when raising our children.

In many two-parent households, parents find it difficult to 'parent on the same page.' Often this may be due to the parenting styles, or values and expectations being different, as well as different experiences from upbringing which has shaped current parent responses.

When there is a co-parent involved, but you are having a difficult time with co-parenting, here are some suggestions. Try to agree on one or two parent goals that both parents view as important. This stage may require each parent to give a little and be willing to compromise. Try to avoid judging the other parent too harshly. Try to separate personal feelings about the other parent (which may be challenging) and instead try to work with the other person for the best interest of the child.

There will be situations where this is not always possible, and in those circumstances, the following may apply:

a. Avoid talking badly about the other parent in front of the child.

b. When possible, show support of the other parent.

c. Reinforce to the child that both parents care about the child, even though the parenting decisions or approaches may be different.

We have found that one of the first questions asked by an individual ending a relationship with a co-parent is, "How will this impact my children?" Dush, Kotila, and Schoppe-Sullivan (2011) research looked at predictors of supportive co-parenting when a relationship ends. The study did have limitations, but the conclusions were something that we have seen in our practices. Prior to and during any dissolution of a relationship, the parents' ability to co-parent effectively and cooperatively appears to increase positive outcomes for children. So, as we mentioned before, it may not look like what you believe is a typical co-parent situation, but there are ways to co-parent outside of the box.

When Parents Cannot Agree

Have you said or experienced this situation? "My ex and I cannot agree on anything when it comes to the children." These situations present with real and profound difficulties.

If the conflict is at such an intensity that it seems impossible to communicate, ask for the co-parent to join you in meeting someone who will help in productive communication and find ways to co-parent effectively. We have noticed that even the most reluctant individual seems to have a soft spot that will lead them to the process. Here is an example of how one parent was able to connect with the other parent and they found their way to a discussion about co-parenting. *(We understand that this is not always possible.)*

Example Case Study

A father of 5 children was referred by his divorce attorney to seek additional parenting help since the classes taken during the divorce proceeding did not seem to make much change. The father stated that he and his ex-wife agreed that they learned many things about co-parenting during the parenting classes that they were mandated to attend as part of the divorce process. The two decided that they would apply the skills that they had learned, but a year later, the disagreements about the children only seemed to intensify, and the father recognized that he was spending too much time stewing over the situation.

The father came into the first session and was able to give a comprehensive history of the marriage, divorce and the birth of the children. He appeared open and willing to discuss his shortcomings and limitations in the marriage and as a father. He readily identified his goals, which were to be the best parent he could be and have some type of co-parenting experience with his ex-wife.

We suggested that the ex-wife join the sessions and the father said that he believed that his ex-wife would not come as "She does not believe in therapy." The father recalled several times during their relationship, he had suggested seeing someone for counseling, but the ex-wife was reluctant. After the first session, the father decided he would talk with his ex-wife about coming in for a few sessions, just to talk about parenting.

At the second session, the father arrived alone and very disappointed. He felt hopeless about things changing. He and his ex-wife had several arguments during the week. The conflict seemed more intense than before, "If that is even possible," said the father at the end of his explanation of the week's activities. So, we said, "Let's start and perhaps we can revisit getting your ex-wife to join you." The first part of assessment went smoothly, and father was eager to learn how he had developed his own parenting style. When we started identifying values, we asked the father, "Where do you and your ex-wife disagree and where do you agree on the values?" The father was able to identify that he and his ex-wife were aligned with being independent. The father recalled stories about the early years and how the couple dreamed about their children. The stories always seemed to lead to children who

are independent. We said to the father, "That's it! You can still align on being independent and how to develop children that are independent." He smiled and asked, "Do you think that would work?" We responded with it was certainly worth a try, and he may risk a few more fights this week but he could certainly withstand those. The father chuckled out loud and agreed.

We helped the father develop a plan on how to engage with the ex-wife around independence with their oldest child. The oldest child was described as fiercely independent and impulsive. The impulsivity created some poor decision-making skills. At the next session, the father appeared and said his ex-wife agreed to come but may be late. The ex-wife arrived about five minutes late and seemed apprehensive and was quick to say, "I do not believe in therapy."

We were able to start the process with the reluctant spouse by talking about the difficulties with the oldest daughter, and her extreme independence and impulsivity. The ex-wife did not agree with the daughter being impulsive but instead felt she was immature and lacked experiences, and the lack of experience was the reason for her decision-making skills being poor at times.

Most of the session, she was engaged, and it appeared she cared deeply for her children. We ended the session talking about goals the two agreed on for each of the children. They both said it was helpful and would return the following week.

Yep, you guessed it, the next session arrived, and the father arrived alone. He reported that he and his ex-wife left the session being cordial and he had hope again things would change. Within two days, things turned back to the old pattern, and the two were arguing about the children. The ex-wife stated that she would not return to the therapy sessions because she believes therapy is not helpful. During this session, we focused on what we had learned from the one and only joint session, plus what the father knew about his ex-wife. We validated that he was right on target about independence and their oldest child. The discussion then moved to each child and where the two agreed. The father felt that he could move toward his goals by alignment he had with the ex-wife, although they could not share effective communication. Also, he was able to communicate with the children about the differences in the houses and how each parent wanted many of the same things for each child.

Yes, the arguments continued, and the communication was not what either parent really wanted for their relationship, but the father was able to recognize and create his plan without so much anger or frustration and worked out of his definition of co-parenting.

Helpful Hint

Many of our parents have said that when they stopped focusing on the fight and started focusing on process, it seemed to help. They did not seem so drained and exhausted. The "fight" shifted to the work on the process of parenting. Remember back in Chapter 3, we talked about communication and language? Well, here we are again. When you shift the language and the focus, it will help in many situations where the conflict is real.

Caution: Avoid self-criticism and assigning blame to the other parent in this exercise. Identify how things are going in the household currently.

Absentee Parent

What creates a family is individualized and defined by the individuals who come together. We work with families that include grandparents, single mothers or fathers, and relatives, such as aunts or uncles, who have assumed the primary caretaker role. Many single parents feel like they never get a break, and they feel that their burdens are not recognized or spoken of in the two-parent world.

We have seen single parents dealing with families who have less time together due to work and home duties, custody and visitation schedules, as well as children spending time with extended family members. Financial stressors are often experienced in the single-parent home. The struggles may be increased when previously the family had a two-parent income or two-parent presence in the home. Childcare costs are substantial, and these additional financial demands can create more stress in the family. We know the pain and difficulties are real. Many of our single parents feel frustrated that the norm for a household is two parents. If you realize that this is you, take a moment and start the process of shifting out of the comparison thinking. Remember, the difficulties are real, but we find that the comparison, and expectation, to function and exist as a two-person household can lead to frustration.

We encourage all families to build a secure support network. This can be especially important in single-parent households. The support networks may consist of family members or friends, or faith community. We suggest, if you continue to feel overwhelmed and your support network is not meeting your needs, then it might be time to seek assistance from a professional.

Example Case Study

During our work with families, we have had opportunities to work with many single parents, and we know that single parenting occurs for a variety of reasons, sometimes through choice, sometimes not. The single-parent household presents some challenges, and at the same time, some parents find "singledom parenting" advantageous. A notable example is a family that we walked along during the children's emergence into adolescence. The family consisted of 3 children and a single father. The father who entered therapy reported, "Although my children only have one parent, at least our home does not have opposing positions or difference of opinions on how things should look or run. I get to make the decisions." Although the father said he was often overwhelmed with all the household duties and work obligations that he managed daily, the father was able to identify a positive aspect in the situation. We validated the father for his recognition.

The father created his plan with the goals he felt were necessary. At times, the father did question his decisions, but by creating a great support system around him, he was able to find others to share his thoughts and gather trusted advice. The father recognized that some of the people he had initially thought would be in his support network for "purposeful parenting" moved outside of his support network because of difference in values or approaches. Besides, some of the individuals with whom he shared similar values had too much emotional investment into the situation and they could not contribute objectively.

We cannot emphasize enough that we recognize and validate all difficulties and the following exercise is not intended to minimize anyone's experience. Instead, we are asking that individuals start thinking and using language that includes "and" when describing these experiences. This concept involves being open to possibilities by exploring various facets of one's story, rather than getting stuck on one troubling part.

Example Case Study

A grandparent in a single-parent home described Wednesday evenings as the time that she dreaded each week. Wednesday evenings was the time that the children went to visit their other grandparents. The grandparent recognized that she focused on how much she missed the children on Wednesday evenings. She was happy that the other grandparents were involved but did feel at times that she was left doing the heavy lifting in the caretaking responsibilities. The grandparent often had feelings of guilt about the times that she had to work late and could not be at home with the children.

The grandparent worked with us and we started by focusing on using "and," rather than focus on one aspect of the situation. The grandparent began with changing the self-talk language, and before too long the emotional experience started shifting. In the past, the grandparent would describe Wednesday evening as a time of dread and sadness as she missed the children the few hours they were absent. The emotional intensity escalated on weeks that she had to work extra hours on Tuesday evening.

Acknowledging opportunities that grandmother received when the children were not home was our first step. The grandparent recognized that it gave her a chance to get a few chores done in a shorter amount of time, due to fewer interruptions and her procrastination. Plus, she made sure she created a minimum of 15 minutes of time for herself. We described this as any opportunity where she could do something that she enjoyed that gave her pleasure and could be restorative to her physical and emotional demands of the day.

At our last session, the grandparent said she still feels guilty when she works late on Tuesday and continues to miss the children on Wednesday evenings, but feels happy to get those 15 minutes, plus loves the speediness of completing the daily chores. The last we heard from the grandmother, some things have changed, some things remain the same and hump day has taken on an entirely different feel since our work, which she loves.

Reflective Questions

1. Name some positives about being a single parent.

....

....

....

....

2. What is the most challenging aspect of parenting alone?

....

....

....

....

3. As a single-parent, what opportunities are available in your community to support you?

....

....

....

....

4. If you are not aware of any supports, who are three people you could ask about community support?

....

....

....

....

5. Are your goals and expectations in line with the other parent?

....

....

....

....

6. What are differences between your parenting style and the other parent's style?

....

....

....

....

7. What are ways your parenting styles could be more aligned?

....

....

....

....

8. While you may not agree on each front, what are some areas that you each could support one another?

....

....

....

....

Take time to notice change, success and marking movement with ceremonies, even if it is a simple sentence, "I noticed today you…"

LEVEL 5B: PARENTING A CHILD WITH HEALTH ISSUES

How Medical Issues Impact Functioning

Parenting a child with significant health issues are beyond the scope of this workbook. In this section, we have included a few ideas about parenting a child with less severe health concerns. Seek additional advice whenever there are health concerns with a child.

At times, emotional issues and stress can lead to physical complaints and may even compound or trigger health issues. Also, health issues and physical symptoms can also trigger or heighten emotional reactions. Health issues commonly associated with emotional concerns, such as anxiety and depression, can also be headaches, migraines, stomachaches, and irritable bowel syndrome, to name just a few.

Since medical issues can trigger emotional reactions such as anxiety, not only in the child but also in caregivers, work with the child whenever possible to manage his or her pain symptoms rather than over-accommodating or excusing the child from expectations. We have found in our work with families that pain management techniques can often be similar to strategies known to be helpful managing stress and anxiety.

- Create goals based on functioning

- Adopt consistency and structure for accountability for child with these issues

- Be mindful of the purposeful responses versus emotional responses

- Purposeful responses can foster growth and management skills versus reinforcing avoidance for child and other secondary gains

Example Case Study

We worked with a 14-year-old girl several years ago who presented with complex medical issues, specifically stomach and digestive issues. She had been to numerous doctors and hospitals, undergone surgeries, and had missed most of her past seven months of school due to illnesses and doctors' visits. Before becoming ill at 14, she was about to enter her freshman year of high school. She was a high achieving student who placed high expectations on herself. Mom was a single mother who worked a lot. When this child began to experience physical symptoms, Mom and daughter began to spend a lot of time together going to multiple doctor appointments and had increased time at home. When the child was ill, her mother began catering to her and being more in tune with those symptoms. The girl's expectations lowered at school, which further created avoidance, as this was a girl who previously had placed a lot of stress and pressure on herself to perform. Despite multiple efforts from her medical staff, the symptoms did not improve. The school made accommodations for schooling to be conducted at home.

The doctors recommended that she visit our day programs, which involved intensive individual and family therapy for anxiety and other emotional issues, to work on ways to manage the medical symptoms with a psychological therapeutic approach. In a few weeks, she started to feel better. The structure of the day program helped her to not focus on her physical symptoms. The intensive therapy worked on pain management techniques, and therapists taught her ways that stress interacts with physical symptoms. Mom also worked on her responses to her daughter.

After a few weeks of treatment, we sat down with the mother and daughter and discussed reasons the girl was feeling better. She acknowledged that she was afraid to return to her previous life in which expectations were so high and she did not see her mother as much. There was fear of getting better and returning to a life that was 'overwhelming and lonely'- her words.

We worked on creating healthy expectations. Mom built time into her day to spend time with her daughter, and worked to reinforce healthier responses instead of being hyper-focused on the physical symptoms. On days the daughter was not feeling well, she worked on self-care and pain management strategies, and was not permitted to spend time on electronics, especially if she did not meet expectations. This approach continued to provide the right amount of structure and support that the girl needed. We checked in on her a few years later, mom and the daughter reported that she was doing very well.

Another Parent Perspective on the Parenting the Child with Medical Issues

"My son has complex migraines and often needs to rest when he is experiencing symptoms. At times, it is difficult for me to know if he is avoiding stressful situations or is experiencing physical distress. I know that stress can trigger migraines. I have worked with him to manage stress and recognize patterns of avoidance."

~ Roger, father of 4

Whenever a child is displaying concerning behavior relating to medical issues, understand how those behaviors are reinforced. Sometimes, changing a response to the child's behavior may inadvertently alter the behavior exhibited by the child.

For instance, a parent providing excessive reassurance for a child who frequently complains of somatic symptoms, such as headaches or stomachaches, may place unneeded attention on the child's physical symptoms. A more effective response would be, "I am sorry you do not feel well, how could you manage?" Some examples are nutrition, sleep hygiene, or daily self-care. Responses should be caring but also consistent, being cautious not to feed into behaviors that are maladaptive. For instance, if the child is sick, have them rest and practice self-care, as opposed to being on electronics, etc. The goal is to assist the child in growing emotionally and learning to manage his or her emotions in a healthy way.

Whenever there are new, on-going or unusual physical complaints, a parent should always seek medical assistance for a complete physical examination.

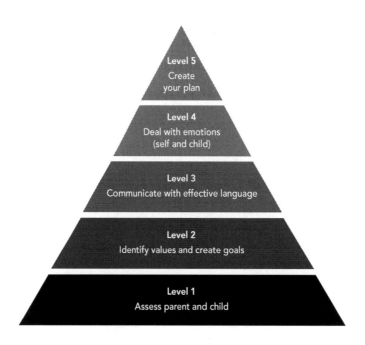

LEVEL 5 SUMMARY

What are the takeaways from this Level 5 Create Your Plan? Take some time to revisit the questions and your answers.

Write any questions or concerns you may want to explore more.

FINAL NOTES: TAKING CARE OF YOU

Parenting takes a tremendous amount of energy. Permitting yourself time to restore and rejuvenate is essential. When the days are long and exhausting, adding another thing to your to-do list may seem daunting and not worth it. Let's revisit the airplane emergency analogy, this time think about the importance of following the guidelines for the oxygen mask; if you run out of the essentials, like oxygen, you are no longer capable of providing care. Self-care is essential to parenting.

We suggest keeping it simple. If the thought of self-care feels outside the realm of possibilities with your schedule and demands, then find the small things that you can do for yourself. When preparing for bed, give yourself a quick facial or massage, or lotion those tired feet a few minutes more with some significant pressure to relieve the stress. Maybe it is a sporting event, or it is that television show you would like to watch. It is important to take a break and spend some time doing something that you enjoy, gives you pleasure, restores you. Hold firm to a hobby or practice that is yours and yours alone. Remind yourself that you deserve these moments because you have worked hard. Positive self-talk during times like these is more impactful than you might realize.

Parenting is not linear, all neat and tidy in a straight line. Some people describe the tough years of parenting as a two-step dance: two steps forward, one step backward and begin...again.

Congratulations to YOU for your commitment to improving the "dance" of parenting. Perhaps this workbook was your first step in enhancing your child's coping skills or the beginning of a smoother morning routine. Awesome. Do not stop the dance. Do not stop working on improvements. Do not stop investing in yourself and your child.

And when challenges come again (and they will), reach out and keep reaching until you find help.

RESOURCES

While we cannot possibly know every community resource, below is a list of national resources, types of community resources you can research in your area, and online social support resources.

Online Resources for Professionals and Families

Essentials for Parenting Toddlers and Preschoolers:
https://www.cdc.gov/parents/essentials/structure/index.html

Supporting the Mental Health of children and youth of separating parents:
https://www.ncbi.nlm.nih.gov/pmc/articles/PMC3804638/

Encyclopedia ~ Scientific knowledge on early childhood development, from conception to age five:
http://www.child-encyclopedia.com/

Positive Behaviors Intervention and Supports - Office of Education Special Education Programs Technical Assistance Center:
http://www.pbis.org/

Relocation and Co-Parenting, The challenge of co-parenting over long distances:
https://www.psychologytoday.com/us/blog/co-parenting-after-divorce/201310/relocation-and-co-parenting

REFERENCES

The A-Team. (n.d.). Retrieved July 13, 2018, from
https://tvtropes.org/pmwiki/pmwiki.php/Series/TheATeam

Alder, S. L. (n.d.). Goodreads. Retrieved from Shannon L. Alder quotes:
https://www.goodreads.com/author/quotes/1391130.Shannon_L_Alder

Atkins, S. (n.d.). Retrieved June 2018, from Sue Atkins The Parenting Expert:
https://sueatkinsparentingcoach.com/2013/09/the-sue-atkins-inspiring-sunday-saying-53/

Barron, C. "Hands-off parenting for Resourceful, Resilient Children. When the best support is less
support." Psychology Today. April 28, 2016.

Berk, L. E. (2013). Child Development. Upper Saddle River: Pearson.

Branden, N. The Six Pillars of Self Esteem (New York: Bantam Books, 1994).

Bradberry, T., & Greaves, J. (2012). Emotional Intelligence Appraisal -
Me Edition. PsycTESTS Dataset.

Brown, J., & Brown, J. (2017). Hate list. New York: Little, Brown.

Campos JJ, Frankel CB, Camras L. On the nature of emotion regulation.
Child Development. 2004;75:377–394

Carroll, L. (2016). Alice's adventures in Wonderland. Strawberry Hills, N.S.W.:
ReadHowYouWant Classics Library.

Cognitive. (n.d.). Retrieved from https://www.merriam-webster.com/dictionary/cognitive

Cowley, M. (1949, January 10). Mister Papa. LIFE, 26(2). 90.

Culp, J. (2018, April). Early Intervention Key to Positive Outcomes for Children with LD. Retrieved from
Lawrence School: https://www.lawrenceschool.org/news-post/~post/early-intervention-key-to-positive-
outcomes-for-children-with-ld-20151105

Dush, C. M., Kotila, L. E., & Schoppe-Sullivan, S. J. (2011). Predictors of Supportive Coparenting After
Relationship Dissolution Among At-Risk Parents. Journal of Family Psychology : JFP : Journal of the
Division of Family Psychology of the American Psychological Association (Division 43), 25(3), 356–365.
http://doi.org/10.1037/a0023652

Dweck, C. S. (2016). Mindset. New York: Ballantine Books.

Greathouse, J. (2011, July 29). Decision Making 101 - Defining Your Values Makes Most Decisions Easy.
Retrieved July 13, 2018, from
http://www.businessinsider.com/decision-making-101-defining-your-values-makes-most-decisions-
easy-2011-7

Greenberg, B. "How to Raise Resilient Kids." U.S News Health Report. February 27, 2017.

Hutyra, H. (n.d.). 109 Powerful Margaret Thatcher Quotes That Will Give You Chills. Retrieved
July 13, 2018, from http://www.keepinspiring.me/margaret-thatcher-quotes/

Jones, C. (2017, August 29). *How I Became an Adult by Raising a Child.* Retrieved July 13, 2018, from https://www.goalcast.com/2017/08/29/became-adult-raising-child/

Lochner, R. (2018, January 25). *"Every Obstacle is Destroyed...* Retrieved July 13, 2018, from http://ricklochner.com/every-obstacle-destroyed/

Marano, H. E. (2010, July 1). *Oh, Brother!* Retrieved July 13, 2018, from https://www.psychologytoday.com/us/articles/201007/oh-brother

Matto, H. C. (2014). *Daniel J Siegel,*
The developing mind: How relationships and the brain interact to shape who we are.
2nd ed. Qualitative Social Work: Research and Practice, (1).

Michelon, P. (2013, April 22). *What is the combined effect of physical and mental training?*
Retrieved July 13, 2018, from
https://sharpbrains.com/blog/2013/04/18/what-is-their-combined-effect-of-physical-and-mental-training/

Morin, A. *"13 Things Mentally Strong Parents Don't Do. Psychology Today. September 28, 2017.*

Mortenson, G. (2010). *Stones Into Schools: Promoting Peace with Education in Afghanistan and Pakistan.* East Rutherford: Penguin Books.

Nichols, R. G. (1980). *The Struggle To Be Human. ILA Convention, (p. 7). Atlanta.*

Oolup, C., Brown, J., Nowicki, E., & Aziz, D. (2015). *The Emotional Experience and Expression of Anger: Children's Perspectives. Child and Adolescent Social Work Journal, (3).*

Riggs, R. (Ed.). (2011, January 23). *Schoolhouse Rock Conjunction Junction.* Retrieved July 13, 2018, from https://www.youtube.com/watch?v=NWBO9NAYm-U

Saarni, C., Campos, J. J., Camras, L. A., & Witherington, D. (2006). *Emotional development: Action, communication, and understanding. In W. Damon & R. M. Lerner (Series Eds.) & N. Eisenberg (Vol. Ed.), Handbook of child psychology: Vol. 3. Social, emotional and personality development* (6th ed., pp. 226 –299). New York: Wiley

Schwartz, Mel. *"Raising Relient Children: The Key to a Happy and Successful Life for your Children".* Psychology Today. Februaury 2, 2015.

Siegel, D. (2001). *The Developing Mind: How Relationships and the Brain Interact to Shape Who We Are.* New York: Guilford Press.

Smith, N. M. (2014, January 14). *Christian Slater: Harrison Ford smooched me at the Golden Globes.* Retrieved July 13, 2018, from https://www.theguardian.com/tv-and-radio/2016/jan/14/christian-slater-harrison-ford-kiss-golden-globes-mr-robot

Uber, T. (Ed.). (2013, February 14). *I'm just a bill.* Retrieved July 13, 2018, from https://www.youtube.com/watch?v=l6MinvU93kl

Zimmer, B. J. (2003). *Reflections for Tending the Sacred Garden.* Lincoln: iUniverse, Inc.

MEET THE AUTHORS

JACQUELINE (JACKIE) RHEW, LCPC, CADC earned her Master of Clinical Psychology from Capella University and her BSW from Valparaiso University. Jacqueline has had a broad range of experience in hospital, educational, and private practice settings, both locally and internationally. Jacqueline has co-authored this toolkit along with several other publications in her over 25 years of treating the whole person. Jacqueline's expertise lies in a multitude of areas such as school refusal, eating disorders, self-injury, substance abuse, gaming addictions, grief issues, trauma, depression, and anxiety. Jacqueline has served both adolescents and adults by the using specific techniques and teachings through individual, family and group therapy. Jacqueline has had proven success through the use of dialectical behavioral therapy, rational emotive behavior therapy, cognitive behavioral therapy, narrative therapy, exposure response prevention, and relational therapy during the therapeutic process. She is an expert in her field specifically consulting with schools, family agencies and mental health hospitals.

As the co-founder of the Center for Emotional Wellness of the Northwest Suburbs, she is called upon by hundreds of school districts both locally and internationally for consulting staff in order to better serve their youth. Jacqueline serves as a clinical liaison for AMITA Health Alexian Brothers Behavioral Health Hospital. She previously served as Assistant Director for the School Anxiety/School Refusal Program; a program she was instrumental in creating and developing. Jacqueline has facilitated 300-plus workshops for professionals and parents, both locally and nationally on topics ranging from anxiety, school refusal, parenting, and self-injury. She continues to be a sought after keynote speaker due to her expertise in her field. She has been featured on Chicago ABC and CBS for her exemplary work and insight. She was interviewed on the treatment of adolescents struggling with avoidant school behaviors as well as bullying. Jacqueline was recently interviewed and quoted on parenting by several newspapers and magazines, including the Chicago Tribune, the Daily Herald, and the Chicago Parent.

ROBIN BOGGS CHOQUETTE, Psy.D. earned a BS in Psychology from Eastern Kentucky University, and Master of Clinical Psychology and Doctorate of Clinical Psychology from Illinois School of Professional Psychology. She has trained in educational, community mental health, hospital and private practice settings. Robin continues to train and enhance her expertise in the field of performance psychology.

Dr. Choquette's practice, Elite Performance Counseling, Inc., is a testament to her vision of building trustworthy and respectful relationships with her clients and community. Robin works with individuals from preteen through older adulthood in individual psychotherapy, family therapy (including parenting strategies), couples therapy, and skill seminars. In addition to her general psychological services, Dr. Choquette consults with a specialized emphasis on performance enhancement for athletes, musicians, artists, corporate executives, and business leaders to help them reach peak performance in their professional and personal lives. She works with youth sporting teams, traveling clubs, and organizations on the mental game of athletics.

Robin is the recent past president of the Exchange Club of Naperville, a service club which has donated over $18 million to area agencies. She consults, volunteers, and has served on the board of directors of several other agencies. She is a member of her local Chamber of Commerce, and is a member of several committees, including the Speakers Bureau and Women in Business. Dr. Choquette is described as an individual with unmatched commitment and problem-resolution skills with a reputation as a direct and approachable professional with impeccable integrity and ethics. Dr. Choquette is committed to respecting the principles, sensitivity, diversity and multicultural background of her clients.

ADDITIONAL NOTES

This area is intended for reflections, journals or notes that you wish to keep. This may be a place that you come back to now and again to reflect on the progress being made.

Made in the USA
Lexington, KY
13 September 2018